ROUTES
to ROOTS

A Collection of
"Tracing Your Roots"
Columns from the
Kitchener-Waterloo Record
1993-1997

Ryan Taylor

Published by: Global Heritage Press
158 Laurier Avenue
Milton, ON, Canada L9T 4S2
1-800-361-5168
Tel: (905) 875-2176
Fax: (905) 875-1887
http://www.globalgenealogy.com

ISBN: 0-9682524-0-0

Printed on acid-free paper and bound in Canada.

for rych mills

who loves books even more than I do
and who enjoys pointing me
down obscure routes of his own finding

Acknowledgements

Over the past four and a half years of writing the "Tracing Your Roots" column in the *Kitchener-Waterloo Record*, I have been encouraged and assisted by a great many kind friends and interested strangers. The column has provided me with the means to see 'behind the scenes' at many libraries and archives, and to talk professionally with my colleagues in the heritage business whom I might never have met otherwise. In addition, the public face of a newspaper columnist allows other people to feel they can approach them to ask questions or discuss issues. I have enjoyed meeting many interesting genealogists in this way. I well remember one evening in Goderich when a stranger told me she had a scrapbook of all the columns which had appeared to that time. It is humbling to think that there are those who value what I write so much.

First expressions of gratitude must go to Carol Jankowski, my editor at the *Record*, who welcomed me there and whose upbeat attitude of encouragement has made every problem seem small. Her colleague John Roe helped my first thoughts of this column grow into a reality.

Many friends opened doors, made suggestions or simply told me to get going with the ideas which have come to me over these years. I want particularly to thank Frances Hoffman, Ron Lambert, Rose Anne Fournier, Steve Myers, Curt Witcher, Georgina Green, Sandy and Rob Lofthouse, Debbie Virkutis and Ian Easterbrook. As always, the telephone reference staff of the Kitchener Public Library have been helpful and efficient.

For the actual creation of this book from scattered columns, I am grateful to rych mills for the use of his files and to Patricia J. Kauk of the Kitchener library for prompt attention to an SOS.

The book was named by Jennie Schmidt with a contribution from David McDonnell.

Fort Wayne, Indiana
July 1997

Introduction

The "Tracing Your Roots" column began in the *Kitchener-Waterloo Record* in March, 1993 and has continued since then. It was, at first, a weekly feature appearing on Saturdays. It later moved to Tuesdays and became twice-a-month. The selection of columns which is included in this volume represent those which continue to offer something to readers (many of the others were ephemeral). If necessary, I have offered updates or additional comments in italics at the end of the column. The information may have been silently updated to reflect 1997 prices or addresses.

In some cases, only part of the column has been reprinted. Usually, the columns have been given in chronological order, but a few have been excerpted and printed with another column on the same topic, because they complement one another.

There is no contents list at the front of the book. I have often been asked for a complete list of the columns by people searching for one in particular; this list is given at the end. Columns reprinted in the book in whole or in part are marked with an asterisk (*) in this list. This is followed by a general subject index.

The initial essay, "Genealogists and Libraries", is printed here for the first time.

Neither the newspaper column nor this reprinted version is a handbook to genealogical research. However, it does offer some routes to help those tracing their roots.

Genealogists and Libraries

Genealogists doing serious research inevitably have to use libraries as a principal source of information. This includes their own local public library and many others far afield, including those in the area where ancestors lived and also large genealogical libraries with collections that will help the work progress.

After three decades of using libraries in my own research and acting on the other side of the desk assisting others, I am convinced that many genealogists simply skim along the surface of most libraries' collections. They could find a great deal more if they exploited these resources fully.

Looking at Libraries: Public libraries are funded by tax dollars, largely from the area in which they are located, but perhaps by higher levels of government as well. Some libraries which you will use are privately maintained by endowments, societies or corporations.

Not all libraries operate in the same way. Although they do have similarities (catalogues, reference tools), they vary considerably in how they use these. For our purposes, the most important variation lies in their attitudes toward genealogical research.

Even twenty years ago, most libraries viewed genealogists as outside their realm of interest. They were, at best, people with narrow interests whom libraries served only as a fringe of society; some librarians regarded genealogists as cranks. There are still those who do.

However, genealogy is now one of the most popular hobbies in North America and every public library will now feel some obligation to provide services to genealogists. Some will have the money to dedicate considerable sections of their space for family history research; small ones will be confined to a shelf of reference materials.

You will come to know your own public library well. Get to know the staff, the layout of the building and every area of the collection which will help you. This concerns not merely the shelves which contain the usual genealogy books (church records, census indexes, tax records and cemetery transcriptions), but also bibliographies, general almanacs or directories, telephone books and so on.

Most of what I am going to say is pointed at your visits to libraries you do not know so well. In your home library, you have plenty of time to explore, to chat with the librarians and otherwise find what you need. When you are visiting far from home, every minute counts, so you should use your time wisely.

Visiting Libraries: before making a library visit, write or make a telephone call and ask for brochures outlining library services, hours of opening and special rules. Be sure to specify you are coming to do genealogical research, in case there is a special room for those resources, which is only open at limited times. Study the materials in advance. If you arrive at the library to find it closed, you have only yourself to blame if you have not called ahead.

To obtain library addresses and telephone numbers quickly, consult *The American Library Directory*. This includes public, private and academic libraries and Canadian libraries are listed in their own section. This book is available in most public libraries.

Even more quickly, you might be able to access the library via its website on the Intenet (see below).

A book which will help those making genealogical excursions in Ontario is *Large Genealogical Collections in Ontario Libraries and Archives* (Ontario Genealogical Society, 1994) which provides information for potential visitors.

When you arrive, begin by locating the reference desk which serves genealogical clients and greeting the librarian on duty. Tell the librarian that you are new to the system and ask for a quick tour or orientation. Some large libraries may have a handout map of the department, or a video describing their services.

Describe the first questions you want to answer and wait for suggestions on how to begin.

Asking questions in a library is an easy process. The reference librarian has been professionally trained for the task. It is important that you remember that the librarian has no interest in your family history, however. Simply ask the question, giving only the detail that is required to understand what you want. Then listen carefully to the suggestions that are made. You might want to make notes. Despite appearances to the contrary, the librarian is almost certainly busy (with both other customers and background duties) and cannot spend a lot of time with you either chatting about your research situation or doing the work for you.

I suggest you do not try to do too much at once. If you have prepared for your trip in a sensible way, you will have a list of the questions you want to work on. Systematically go down your list ticking each one off as you do; this way you accomplish what you want without wasting time.

The librarian will probably suggest some materials you have already consulted. Listen to the suggestions anyway, for there may be new editions of the books, a new index or some aspect of the material you did not realize was there. (An example: I frequently deal with people who have consulted the 1901 census but say they do not know when their ancestors arrived in Canada; this information is given, by the ancestors themselves, in that census.) It is not helpful to say to the librarian, "I looked there already, there's nothing there."

As for the resources which are suggested and you do not know, you will either find that they are pointed out to you, or you will have to consult the catalogue to locate them on the shelf.

The Catalogue: library catalogues are intimidating to most of us, even to some librarians. The people who create them are known (in the library world) as 'technical services' librarians because the catalogues are formulated according to certain rules. To make it easier to move from library to library (and to facilitate library cooperation), catalogues are created using rules laid down by international cooperative bodies so they will be the same. The national libraries of Canada, the United States and the United Kingdom all participate in fomulating the rules.

This means that you can learn how to use a catalogue in your home library and then (with luck) go to many other libraries, large and small, and understand how to find books there too. Having said that, I have to warn you that computer catalogues are different everywhere, but they all still follow the international rules. Here are some suggestions regarding catalogues:

If the library you visit has a card catalogue, you probably know how to use it from days of instruction at school. Card catalogues are now found mostly in small libraries. They have cards for the book's author/s, title/s and subject/s. These may be filed in one alphabetical sequence or broken up into sections (usually Author & Title, and Subject). Books can have more than one title, because the publisher has called the book one thing on the title page, another on the cover, another on the spine. The catalogue should have a card for each possible title.

Most sizable libraries now have an automated (computer) catalogue. Do not be nervous about it. Although there are many formats for these catalogues, most of them have been created with the idea that people can teach themselves how to use them by following the simple instructions on the screen. It will still be possible to find the book you want by searching using the author's name, a title or a subject. Again, if the book has four titles on its various parts, each of them should be available in the catalogue.

Sometimes people who work with technology every day have developed a shorthand way of referring to it. They may call the catalogue terminal an 'OPAC' (for on-line public access catalogue), for instance. If the librarian begins to do this, and you do not understand what is being said, ask that they speak in simpler language. This is a sensible and legitimate thing to do, so do not feel embarrassed or think that you may appear 'stupid'. Everything concerned with library catalogues can be explained in language that everyone can understand. It is important that you feel comfortable using this important library tool.

Simply sit down at the terminal and read what it says. If you are looking for a particular book, you will have an author or title, Make the choices indicated on the screen, type in what is asked, and you will find the answer popping up before you know it.

If you cannot understand how it works, ask the reference librarian for assistance. The library may even have a brochure which explains the commands you need for their system. If not, the librarian will give you a short lesson.

Books in libraries are arranged on the shelf in numerical order, using a numbering code which ensures that everything on a similar subject ends up sitting together. The code for an single book is known as a 'call number'. From the catalogue, you take the call number and then can find the book on the shelf. You can search yourself or ask for assistance if you need to.

Some libraries cannot keep all their books on the shelves which the public sees for reasons of space or convenience. In that case, you may have to fill out a slip and then wait while the book is retrieved by library staff, either to your desk or to a pickup area.

If you find this kind of system inconvenient, it is not useful to complain to the librarian. The various rules which are in place in large institutions have been conceived to make the place run smoothly. It is better to learn the rules and then follow them carefully; trying to circumvent them simply wastes everyone's time and probably will lead to resentment on the part of both yourself and the library staff. This includes rules on book use, the price of photocopying, eating in the library, using pens in archives or limits to the amount of material you can have on your desk at one time. While you are waiting for your books to come, cruise around in the catalogue looking for other materials, or skim the bookshelves in the public area to see if you can find something helpful that you did not know about before. You can also time your requests throughout the day to ensure you always have something on your desk to work with.

When you use the catalogue, the most useful way to access materials may well be through the subjects, because you will not know exactly which books contain the information you require.

When books are catalogued, they are assigned subject headings from an approved list. This is done to ensure that when you visit different libraries, you will always know what subjects to consult and also that the same headings are always used within the library. The usual list is formulated by the Library of Congress in Washington (although very small libraries may use a simpler list called Sears). The National Library of Canada has additional headings for Canadian topics.

To explain this, say you are looking for material on church records. You may look under 'Church records' but someone with a Lutheran background may think of 'Church books' or even 'Kirchenbuch' and someone else may use 'Register'. Then there are various kinds of church records: baptisms, marriages, burials, mission circle minutes, lists of members. To ensure that all this material comes under one heading, libraries use 'Church records and registers' as the approved heading. You should also be aware that many libraries have a supplemental list of headings for local topics which are not known in Washington or Ottawa. Ask the librarian about theirs.

If you are not sure what the approved heading might be for what you want, ask the librarian. A copy of the subject headings list may well be sitting near the catalogue for consultation. Always be as specific as you can when looking in the catalogue. For instance, if you are looking for records from King Street Baptist Church in Preston, look under 'King Street Baptist', under 'Preston', under 'Church records and registers - Ontario - Preston' or under 'Baptists,' until you find what you want.

Different kinds of books: what you are hoping to find are actual records which include your family's information. However, you may have to go through some preliminary steps before you reach that resource. Take the time to cruise the catalogue looking for background materials which may help you. The first of these is a handbook on how to do genealogy in the area where your family lived. This may be as broad as a provincial guide or as narrow as something for the town or village you are visiting.

The handbook will describe what is available, what form it is in, where it is; it may even tell you that sad but important news: what has been lost or destroyed.

Every area has some quirky local resources created by well-meaning people but which do not fit into ordinary categories. These may be books but are often archival resources in files or scrapbooks. The only way to learn about these resources is to read about them in a handbook or be directed to them by the librarian. You should always remember that the librarians who work in this area every day have specialized knowledge which you do not; listen to the advice they give you. An example of this kind of resource is the vast collection of files created by Keith Matthews when he was gathering information about the fishing families of Newfoundland. These files have never been published, but are all available to the public at the Maritime History Archive in St. John's.

Handbooks may be geographical in outlook (there are published genealogical handbooks for the Atlantic Provinces, Ontario, Manitoba and Alberta), about a specific library (such as *The Library*, about the big Family History Library in Salt Lake City), or about a certain topic (such as John Humphrey's *Understanding and Using Baptismal Records*). None should be neglected.

Bibliographies are lists of books. You may be tempted to bypass them as dull or too time-consuming. However, reading a bibliography can help you find books which you did not know existed, and which contain family information you cannot find elsewhere. **The big step in research in genealogical books is not looking in the book itself, but in finding the book in the first place.**

Libraries stock large numbers of bibliographies of many kinds. For family history purposes, you should look for those which list reference tools for specific areas (for instance, Stuart Raymond's bibliographies for individual English counties), lists of family histories published either in a certain place or a certain year, or collections of books located in a particular library. You may find exactly what you want, but also learn that it is available only in a certain library hundreds of miles away. Without the bibliography, you might never have learned of its existence.

A friend of mind was selling a bibliography he had published at a genealogy conference. A woman bought one, scurried out the door, looked inside and then came back in to say that it did not have anything she wanted. Would he buy it back? He would not, but she had no trouble selling it to someone else minutes later. That was too bad, for most bibliographies are too complex to appreciate everything they contain in a few minutes. No doubt she missed something that could have helped her.

One very handy kind of bibliography which we should always look at are those in local histories. People who write these local books have often consulted very obscure publications which they will include in their list of reference sources. The next time you look in a local history, take a moment to scan the bibliography (or footnotes, if that is all the book has), to ensure you do not miss some tiny source which is not listed anywhere else.

Libraries are also very fond of books which contain lists of other materials. These will provide you with ideas for finding information not easily located elsewhere. In addition, these kind of books are often not the sort you will want to have at home (because they are expensive and take up a lot of space). The library is the perfect place to house (and pay for) these resources, and they are always there for you to use. An example of this kind of book is Mary Bond's magnfiicent three volumes which detail the directories of Canada (city, county or regional listings); one volume of the set is devoted to an index which tells you which fat directory contains the tiny place where your family lived (over 23,000 entries). The set costs over $200, so you do not want it at home, but most Canadian public libraries will be glad to see you using their copy.

One giant bibliography which you may want to know about is the database compiled by OCLC in Columbus, Ohio. Hundreds of libraries (including the National Library of Canada, the Library of Congress and the Allen County Public Library, all with huge genealogy collections) contribute their catalogues to this database which performs many functions for the library world; the most important of these for you is that they have an on-line searching function called FirstSearch. You have access to the whole database, and can use it to find all the bibliographic details about any book which interests you, and what libraries own it. Ask your local librarian if they have access to FirstSearch. If they do not have it, a large public library or academic library nearby may instead.

In the general reference area are a great many books which genealogists need but may not know about. Once again, ask the librarian. The most prominent of these are directories of addresses, of many different kinds. I often hear people plaintively asking how to get in touch with this person or that institution. The library probably has the answer. If you have an 'unanswerable question', before you print it in your local genealogical newsletter or call a chat show to ask, consult the reference desk at the library. The librarian there probably knows.

Interlibrary loan: perhaps the best library service which genealogists do not use is interlibrary loan. Libraries nowadays have a heavy emphasis on cooperation, because every library cannot collect every book. There are too many published each year. So, some libraries specialize, some have the space to keep certain kinds of old books while others feel able to discard them.

However, all libraries can lend books to one another. If your local library does not have something you need, you can often borrow it from a library far away. The service of locating the book you want and arranging for it to be shipped to your hometown is something your local public library does for you.

To arrange for this service, all you have to do is determine that the book exists. This may not be as easy as it sounds, and you cannot simply go to the library and ask them to bring in the printed registers of St. George's Anglican Church in Harriston unless you can prove that St. George's registers really have been printed.

The information which the library requires is the author, title and year of publication. If you know the publisher, that is good, but is not necessary. You should also realize that not all books have an author who is named in the text; in that case, you need not name him.

You may not have the proper information. You will have to tell the librarian where you heard of the book; if you found it referred to in another book, bring along a photocopy of the relevant page.

There are ways of trying to discover the full author, title and year of publication. You might find it in a bibliography, or by looking in another library's catalogue on the Internet. The best way (and the one which libraries themselves use) is to look in the OCLC database which I mentioned earlier.

Once you have determined the book you want to see, then simply fill out the request form at your local library and then sit back and wait for it to arrive. Many people think that they have to tell their library where the book can be found. That is the library's job. Many more libraries probably carry the book than you know, and the interlibrary loan department at your library will determine which of these is most convenient for them. You should also keep in mind that many libraries do not lend their genealogical reference material, but your own library will work to find one that does.

Some books cannot be lent, because they are too fragile or too rare. Do not give up. These kinds of books are often available for loan in microform. Many have been reprinted in editions other than the one you requested. Also, a great deal of archival material in microform can also be borrowed in this way. Ask for the librarian's advice.

Sometimes you may only wish to see a certain page (very common for items found in Filby's passenger lists index). In that case, the interlibrary loan people can request a photocopy of the page instead of the whole book.

In fact, Curt Witcher advises you to include your specific reason for needing to see a book on the interlibrary loan form. It may be that the lending library will not send the book, but "may be quite happy to copy a citation, a crest, an index, and even a chapter or two in place of lending the book."

Some libraries (often large academic institutions) charge for lending their books through this system. Your own library may also have a fee. These amounts are nominal only, and never cover the whole cost of the lending process.

Genealogists sometimes tell me their hometown librarian tries to avoid interlibrary loan. Almost always I find that these librarians work in very small libraries. They simply do not know how to use the system for their clients' advantage. Be firm and insist they try for you, because their library will benefit from their increased knowledge.

At times of the year when people rarely travel (such as winter) or if you are confined to home by health or family events, you can still pursue your research using interlibrary loan. In talking to genealogists over the years, I realize few of them take advantage of this wonderful service. They are missing a great deal of information and useful learning.

Microforms: much genealogical material is now available in microform (either microfilm or microfiche). Microfilms are on reels; microfiche are sheets or cards. Surprisingly enough, I still hear people complaining about having to use microforms. They should consider how convenient it is to have these archival materials available in many places instead of just one, and how much better it is to use a vast collection of old papers on microfiche than to have to carefully go through them by hand. In fact, it is unlikely we would be able to see the originals even if they were not on microform, because they would disintegrate under the constant use.

More archival material is being transferred to microform every year. This means it can be made available on interlibrary loan. The most obvious example of this is the Church of Jesus Christ of Latter-day Saints Family History Centers, which are branches of the Family History Library in Salt Lake City. They bring thousands of microfilmed records to individual researchers from all over the world, people who have never been to Utah. Closer to home, many records of the Archives of Ontario can now circulate to people elsewhere.

Better yet, much of this material can be bought by individual libraries or people. A good example of this is the Wesleyan Methodist baptismal records of nineteenth century Ontario. They occupy only four reels of microfilm. Using them can be quite difficult because of their arrangement in the original ledgers, but now many libraries both in Ontario and abroad can make them available for leisurely research. With the addition of many volumes of local indexes to these records, the information contained in them has become quite accessible.

Microfilm readers are available in even the smallest libraries now (usually for reading local newspapers and census). Printers for microfilm are also commonplace and have become much easier to use in the past few years.

New technology: information can also be found on newer technology. Most commonly, library users might find **CD-ROMs** or material available via on-line computers.

CD-ROMs are small disks, similar to the compact disks on which you play music at home. They contain thousands of bits of information which can be read on special computers. Your own computer at home may have this capability, in which case you may be buying **CD-ROMs** yourself. Certainly libraries are purchasing **CD-ROMs** in great numbers because they contain vast amounts of information stored in a small space and are available much more cheaply than large printed books. Ask your librarian to explain how the machines work, and what kinds of information they have available in this format. You should familiarize yourself with this technological innovation because increasing kinds of resources will soon be available in this way, perhaps in this way only.

Most people will also have heard about resources which can be found on-line, probably via the Internet. I cannot possibly begin to explain the Internet in a small amount of space, but suffice it to say that you can now log on a computer in your local library (or at home) and within seconds find yourself searching in a database across the country or over the ocean.

Most large libraries now have websites which you may visit, which will explain their services and collections. They may even be able to link you directly to their catalogue, so you can study it from home. People with technological interests have also created their own websites. They usually have linked their sites to others: their friends, institutions they like, pages for business enterprises or ideas. Once you begin travelling from one site to another, you may find yourself sailing for hours in a dazzling array of information!.

Many of these individuals have made databases of their own, creating indexes, lists or simply dumping in material created by others. The results can be impressive, when one connects with a list which turns out to contain information about your own family. It may be that you think you can do genealogy without ever leaving your home.

Sites on the Internet can be very useful in providing us with guides to resources. However, they should not be seen as resources in themselves. If you find data about your ancestor in a website, certainly make a note of it. Then look at the site carefully to determine where the data came from and how dependable it is. To be trustworthy, it must state where the original details were found. Then, you must go back to that original source to verify that everything you found on the Internet matches the first source, and that nothing has been omitted. This will require leaving the Net and actually visiting a library or archives. If you create a genealogy based totally on information you gleaned on the Net, you will be building a house of cards.

Use the Internet as a guide to what is available, to information you may not be easily able to find elsewhere. It is not a source in itself. As the Internet grows (which it does every day, to an astonishing extent), it will become more and more a part of our research environment.

Many libraries now have Internet terminals. Some of them are available for a fee, others for free. If you have not tried the Internet, I urge you to do so, simply because it is so important now for people who are searching for information. Once again, I find that people are often afraid of the Internet because it is new and potentially so complex. However, if you ask for assistance you will be sure to find someone eager to show you around. If the librarians cannot do this, I am sure you will be able to locate a computer junkie in your local genealogy group who will be glad to show you the way.

Some hints: once you have begun your exploration of libraries, you will find that the more you know about them, the more you find. Many of the researchers I meet come to the library with a mindset which guarantees their searches will be unsuccessful.

Keep your mind open. There are sure to be resources you have never heard about. Welcome them. Consider that you may have made a mistake or missed something when you looked at some resource in your early days as a genealogist. It might be a good idea to look at it again. Inevitably you will find information which contradicts something you found before, or what your Aunt Muriel told you. Before you dismiss the new information out of hand, consider both sources carefully and wonder which one is right.

I often hear people say, "But it has to be here!" I want to ask them, "Why?" but librarians are not allowed to do this. There are no guarantees. The information you want so desperately may be lost, may have burned in a fire or been eaten by rats, may have been miscopied by the book's compiler. Or more likely, it may simply never have been there in the first place, because your ancestor neglected to register the birth (or the deed, or the probate). You may think that saying, "It has to be here!" is simply showing a brave optimism, but it more often sounds like a bull-headed lack of understanding.

It is important to be thorough, of course. Make a note of every text you consult, so you do not end up looking at it again on your next port of call. Examine every book which may possibly contain an answer, if only to confirm that they do not. Take the opportunity to consult with experts, whether they be the authors of books, librarians or people you meet while lingering at the catalogue. One of the grandest things about genealogists is that they are so willing to assist their fellows and share their discoveries.

And do not forget to bring your glasses and do not leave them behind. Or your teeth, for that matter (someone did once, at an archives I know).

The columns start on the next page.

18

Family Stories

Every family has its own stories. Handed down from generation to generation, they tell us something important about ourselves. For the genealogist, they can be useful, if they are used carefully. If the story you have heard begins, "My grandmother would have been the Duke of Northumberland if only she had been a boy," then beware. Stories of lost fortunes and grand families begin in a small way but are puffed up in the telling. Finally they have been told so often, everyone believes the inflated version as the truth.

In fact, stories passed down orally over several generations will have changed. Human memory is such that it changes the details in a story each time it is told, refining and emphasizing new aspects of the tale. Facts are forgotten and changed. The current version may not resemble the original much.

If you are a family historian, you can use these stories but you should not look on them as factual until you can find proof in a written source. Sometimes the story still has a kernel of truth left in them, but you have to find out what that kernel is.

Legends about the origins of families in the New World often begin with three brothers. They come out from Europe and settle in three different places. Three is a common number in mythology, but research shows us that there are usually not three brothers. And there might well be some sisters too.

The yarn about immigrant experiences is a common one. People were miserable on cramped, filthy sailing vessels coming over. They almost starved. They braved cholera in Montreal or typhoid in New York.

In the early days there were few roads. At certain times of the year, they were impassable. Travel was actually easier in winter than in spring or fall. There are many tales of people bound for Waterloo County who walked from Buffalo, the end point of the Erie Canal. In one family they say their ancestor had only 25 cents to his name. He walked, staying with strangers on the way, and reached Berlin with his 25 cents still in his pocket.[†]

Stories such as this stress ingenuity, toughness and strength of spirit. We believe these are the qualities which made our pioneer ancestors survive in the wilderness. We hope they passed the same on to us. That is the reason these stories have been passed down and why we should record them in

---

[†] This story from the Sattler family is told in Rufus Sattler's oral history tape at the Kitchener Public Library.

writing for future generations. Our abilities to remember and hand on stories has diminished in the past couple of generations, because of television and a shortened attention span. Stories written down now will survive for the future.

One tale I have heard many times over the past twenty years, told in my own family, on the Prairies, in Quebec, in Indiana. Everywhere there is a version.

Tom Wilford of Crosshill told me this story about his grandmother Livergood. She was at home with her children, her husband being away. Suddenly a bear put its head in the window of her log cabin, interested in making a meal out of one of the babies. Mrs Livergood took up her broom and attacked the bear. It was startled and quickly left her alone, running into the woods.

Why does this simple tale exist in so many forms and so many places in North America? It illustrates pioneer vitality and the strength of women settlers. To me, it is the Great Canadian Family Story.

(13 March 1993)

Looking At Obituaries

Death notices supply us with a variety of information about family members. Even if you know the date of death already, you should look at the obituary for further clues in your research.

It used to be said that a lady's name appeared in the newspaper only three times in her life: when she was born, when she married and when she died. This was untrue, as social columns detailed who visited who. Accounts of teas and socials not only told who poured but what they wore. And to cap it off, old-style birth notices did not give the baby's (or mother's) name at all. To read them, you would think Dad did all the work.

Of the three, death notices are those which appear most consistently. In the past, births were announced only occasionally, and marriages sometimes, but the death of a resident of the community had the importance of a public event. Everyone wanted to know.

Nineteenth century death notices tend to be very short, two lines or so, giving name, place of death and age. If the deceased was a woman or child, a relative's name would be included. However, if the person was notable in some way—an early settler or very old—more details might be given.

Obituaries as we know them were rarer then, although after World War I became more common for everyone. In older papers, look in the social columns and scan the news items for fuller obituaries. Sometimes they have no heading and you must look carefully.

If you find them, the details given can be surprising for those used to our cut and dried death notices. One I saw recently devoted a paragraph to a description of the grave itself, placed so that there would be room for an extra-large monument, its walls lined with cedar boughs for the funeral.

You can expect to find death date and place, where burial took place, a list of surviving family members and perhaps birth information in an obituary. These notices are good places to look for lost family members. If they survived the dead person or returned for the funeral, their names will be given and their new place of residence. The elusive birthplace of the emigrant ancestor can also be found in death notices, if you are lucky.

The smaller the newspaper, the more likely you will find a full obituary, for a death in a small town was a newsy event. If you find the obituary, look a week later for an account of the funeral, which will have details to enrich your family history.

If you wonder what newspaper to look in for your family's notices, or where to find surviving copies, check J. Brian Gilchrist's *Inventory of Ontario Newspapers 1793-1986*. It is available in many libraries and will direct you to copies of the papers you need.

(17 April 1993)

Writing Genealogical Queries

Asking for help in your family history becomes a necessity after a while. The resource material may be far away or you may be uncertain where to look next. You will find yourself writing a letter to an archives, a family history society or an individual asking for help.

Writing a genealogical query is simple. State what you know, then ask the question.

The trick lies is knowing how to state what you know. For many people, this means writing pages of family history. The person receiving this letter does not have time to read it and may never reply.

Your question should be straightforward. "I am looking for my grandmother's birth date," is a good example. Then you explain where you think she was born, approximately when, and remember to include her name.

I once received a letter which asked, "Please send me my grandfather's gravestone inscription from the Wanner Cemetery." That was all—no name included.

Your own name and address is necessary, preferably typed, but at least printed carefully. Your letter should not ask more than two or three simple questions. Val Greenwood, author of the definitive book on American research, says that genealogical letters must not be more than one page long.

Most genealogical newsletters have a page or more of genealogical queries submitted by society members. They seem to be written in code until you are used to the short forms which are common. If you belong to a society, make sure you take advantage of their queries columns. If they offer two free queries a year, be certain yours get published. Studies have shown that most genealogists turn to the queries first when their newsletter arrives. Everyone hopes to find a long lost cousin with information to share.

The Genealogical Research Directory is an annual which consists entirely of queries. Hundreds of pages long, it offers the chance for worldwide connections. For a small fee, you can submit ten names you are researching. They are published, with your address as a contact. When I placed my ancestral name "Neno" a few years ago, I heard from cousins in San Franciso and New Zealand. Our families had communicated last about 1830. If the GRD interests you, copies are available in the library of the Waterloo-Wellington branch of the Ontario Genealogical Society.

(22 May 1993)

National Archives of Canada

With summer coming, you might want to plan a genealogical research trip. One possible destination is the National Archives in Ottawa.

The National Archives has many resources for research, and the rest of your family can take in the museums and other attractions of the nation's capital.

All available census are in help-yourself bins in the reading room. The Ontario ones are also available locally (at Wilfrid Laurier University library), so you might want to concentrate on something else.

Ships' passenger lists are also on microfilm. You have to know the port of arrival and date to narrow things down, as the films are organized chronologically. With a few days at your disposal, you can search through various lists, looking for your immigrant ancestor.

Before 1900 the most common military records are militia lists. Theoretically all of the fit men of fighting age were eligible for the militia a century ago. The lists of who served in drills and training camps can still be examined in their original form. There are plans for these lists to be published[†], but not for a year or two yet, so you might want to look for an ancestor's name. They are organized by geographical area, so you will need to know where the man lived.

Beginning with the Boer War, there are a variety of military records for searching, and an extensive nominal index which the staff will be glad to explain.

When visiting large archives such as the one in Ottawa, go prepared to spend a number of hours, including some time becoming used to the reading room itself. When you arrive, you will need to obtain a pass, so bring some identification with your address (or a passport).

Once you have a pass, go straight to the genealogical services desk and ask for a quick tour. You will want to browse in the catalogues, looking for family names or place names you know.

Before venturing to Ottawa, prepare ahead by looking at the National Archives section in Angus Baxter's *In Search of Your Canadian Roots*. Write for their free pamphlet on genealogical research in Canada to 395 Wellington Street, Ottawa ON K1A 0N3.

The National Library of Canada's reading room is in the same building as the National Archives. They provide access to everything published in Canada since 1952, and many older materials. They too provide friendly staff to help the new user.

Enjoy your visit to the National Archives reading room—you might find yourself working at the table next to Pierre Berton, as I did.
(29 May 1993)

Tweedsmuir Histories

Local history is an important part of genealogy. As well as looking at personal information about your ancestors, you will want to know more about their community.

[†] Published in 1995 as *Men of Upper Canada*.

Local history was for a long time the lot of amateur historians. The professionals and academics spent their time on big issues of economics and politics. The history of the local blacksmith shop was of no interest.

That changed about twenty five years ago, at the time of the Centennial. Many local histories were published and a new interest was born. Now some of our most distinguished academic historians are also local historians.

One fascinating but little used local history resource is still in the hands of caring amateur historians, however. These are the Tweedsmuir Histories maintained by Women's Institute chapters throughout the province.

The idea to compile area histories was suggested by Susan, Lady Tweedsmuir, wife of a governor-general of Canada. Each group would put together farm, family and village histories of its own area. Much of the work was based on local knowledge, which is essential in history of this kind.

A curator was designated for each Women's Institute chapter and her own enthusiasm and creativity were responsible for the growth of the book. Many of the Tweedsmuirs grew into treasure troves of information and photographs, unique records of their area. The only problem was that there was only one copy, at the curator's house.

Not every Women's Institute chapter had a Tweedsmuir, but many did and with more than 25 groups in Waterloo County alone, that was a lot of information.

You can find biographies of individuals, stories of businesses, road building, bridges and rivers. The histories of farms and buildings are especially useful for family historians, who may find data about their own relations.

Many of the books were microfilmed and copies lodged at the Archives of Ontario. These filmed copies are now available locally at the Kitchener, Cambridge and Elmira libraries. Some of the groups have folded, but their Tweedsmuirs live on in these copies. Some originals are also in libraries. For instance, the Ayr library regularly displays their local Tweedsmuir.

The Tweedsmuir is an organic thing. It keeps growing. If you want to look at current Tweedsmuirs, you must arrange to visit the curator. To determine if there is a Tweedsmuir for an area that interests you throughout Ontario, write to the Federated Women's Institutes of Ontario, 7282 Wellington Road, RR #5, Guelph N1H 6J2.
(19 June 1993)

Update: Look at the Women's Institutes website at http:// www.tdg.ca/ontag/fwio. Tweedsmuirs on microfilm at the Archives of Ontario may now be borrowed on interlibrary loan.

Department of Agriculture Records in the 1850s

People often look for birth, death or marriage certificates before 1869, but they are disappointed. Government registration of these events began July 1, 1869. Previous to that, researchers must depend on church records.

The government of Canada first began trying to keep track of these events by asking clergy to send in annual reports of their baptizing and burying in the 1850s. Marriages were especially important, because a wedding celebrates a civil contract as well as a religious ceremony.

Spurred by the example of the British government, which first registered births, deaths and marriages (or BDMs) in 1837, Canadian civil servants tried to collect these records, treating them primarily as statistics. Because statistics were the responsibility of the Department of Agriculture, this is where the clergy reports were filed.

We might think it odd to find church records among the Agriculture files. Only a limited number were collected before the system fell apart. Another means of recording marriages began in 1858, but the material collected is still at the National Archives of Canada (RG 17 IV 4 vol. 1). It is now available on microfilm.

Records from churches near your ancestors' home may be in this collection. To see what is available, look in Patricia Birkett's *Checklist of Parish Registers at the National Archives* (1986), which should be available in your local public library.

Question: How could my great-great-grandmother be 45 years old in the 1871 census, and in the 1881 census be only 50?—Laurie Strome, Kitchener

Answer: Census takers obtained their information from whomever was home when they called. It could be the parents of the house, but it might have been one of the children, a mother in law or visiting aunt. The information given was only as accurate as the person supplying it.

As well, people in the 19th century often had only a vague idea of how old they were. They did not have a birth certificate to refer to. They rarely had to fill out a form stating their age or birthdate. Many were illiterate.

They knew how old they were and every once in a while revised the age up a year or two. It was rare for adults to celebrate their birthdays, especially the men. In the 1901 census, everyone was obliged to state their birthdate for the census taker. It is surprising how many adults did not know it.
(26 June 1993)

Local Census-Assessment Records

It seems hard to believe, but Waterloo County was once part of the county of Halton.

In the early days of settlement, Upper Canada was divided into administrative districts and then counties. Because our area was on the fringe of settlement, it was governed from far away. The district and county boundaries changed often, as immigrants poured in.

For a long period this area was part of the Gore District, based in Hamilton. It covered a wide territory from Oakville to Brantford and north to the unknown country which is now Wellesley.

The first Canadian census which lists every person's name was taken in 1851. There had been earlier attempts at counting the population in Ontario (in 1842 and 1848), but very little survives of these documents. Family historians wished that there were some earlier records to help us with our research in the 1830s.

A worker at the Archives of Ontario turned up some of these records a few years ago in the archives' basement in Toronto. They are census-assessment records. For our area, some go back as far as 1816.

For each household, the records list the head's name (usually the man of the house), address, how many people lived there, and what agricultural products they made in the previous year. The entry ends with a tax statement.

The descriptions of the families are divided into four categories: men over and under sixteen, women over and under sixteen. In some cases the age divisions are more complex.

The use of these to genealogists is obvious. Since the exact lot number is given, you can locate your ancestors here year by year. The family descriptions enable us to get a picture of the size and composition of the group. The agricultural products list can give us an economic picture of the pioneers.

Since the assessments were done every year, a series of them makes it possible to follow our ancestors as they move around or as they produce more on the farm. The earliest entries (from 1816) are for Waterloo Township. They continue in a broken sequence up to 1840 or so. There are also extensive listings for Wilmot and Woolwich. The listings for Dumfries are much less complete. There are none for Wellesley, which was not officially settled until 1843.

These records cover the period 1820-1840, and the county records begin in the 1850s. There is a gap in the 1840s. These records are unindexed, but the population was small, so looking through the handwritten lists is quick and simple.

The Gore District census-assessments are available at the Archives of Ontario in Toronto. A microfilm copy can be found in the Kitchener Public Library.

(3 July 1993)

Religious Newspapers

Announcing births, deaths and marriages in the newspaper was not as common in the early days. Fewer people could read and write. There were not as many newspapers either.

The earliest newspaper in our area was the *Canada Museum*, first published in 1835. The earliest newspapers here were in German.

Other early local newspapers began in the 1840s, in Galt and Guelph. These papers did have birth, death and marriage announcements, but only a few in each issue. It seems that the reporter for the Canada Museum would go to the local clergy and ask what marriages he had performed recently, then put them in the paper.

There were larger newspapers in the big towns on the lake, Toronto and Kingston. Even more important were the religious newspapers. Each sect had its own publication. It contained religious news, stories and inspirational readings, and announcements. These were usually marriages and obituaries.

People valued their newspapers highly. Since not everyone could afford to buy the paper, they were passed around and read aloud in the family circle. Those living in the country were sent papers by their city cousins.

Modern researchers may not think to look at these religious papers for material on their families, but they should not be neglected. Fortunately, the search has been made easier because the vital notices have been extracted for some of them and published in book form. Donald A. McKenzie has published a series of books indexing these notices from Methodist papers. The

Hamilton Branch of the Ontario Genealogical Society has extracted the Baptist newspaper notices. Both of these series are available at the Kitchener library.

You can find the names and dates of these papers, and current locations, by asking at your church archives.

Sometimes these papers came a great distance, so keep an open mind about which paper might be the one for you. A local couple researching an Elmira family found lengthy obituaries of their ancestors in a church newspaper published in Cleveland, Ohio.

(7 August 1993)

What Church's Records Should I Look In?

The biggest problem in using church records is locating the documents. We may think we know our family's denomination, but I recommend keeping an open mind.

When I ask new genealogists what religion their ancestors were, they often reply, "Protestant." While people of our era may give this vague reply when asked about religion, our ancestors never did. They may not have been churchgoers, but they knew if they were Presbyterians, Methodists or Baptists.

People also say, "My family has always been Methodist." There were many changes in religion over the years. Each time a couple married, they had to choose which church to attend, his or hers. Often the choice was determined by the simple expedient of which denomination had a church in the neighbourhood. While this does not apply to the Roman Catholics, it was a rare family which could drive miles every Sunday to attend the traditional church of their family.

In the early days, churches were few. Ministers travelled from place to place on horseback, holding services in schools, barns and hotels. One of the earliest Lutheran services recorded in Berlin was held on Joseph Schneider's threshing floor. A list of the communicants at that service still exists.

The Methodist circuit which included Wilmot was based in the nearest big centre, Bright. The Anglican missionary in Milton had a parish which covered eleven townships, north as far as Egremont and south to Berlin. It was a huge area which he travelled every few weeks, on horseback through mud and snow. Unfortunately, these early records from Bright and Milton no longer exist.

To locate the circuit records from the area and period which interests you, ask at the church archives. They will have some idea about missionaries in the early settlements. Since these records are often lost, be prepared for disappointment, but make sure you look anyway.

No matter what denomination your ancestors were, look in the records for all Protestant denominations in the early days. If people needed a clergyman, they used the services of whoever was passing. While the baptism of babies might wait for an appropriate time, burials took place immediately, often with only a lay person reading the service. Marriages may or may not have been able to wait. The participants might have travelled to meet the clergyman at his home or a convenient crossroads.

A genealogist said to me recently, "But they *had* to be married in this particular church!" There is no "had to" in genealogy. If the record you want does not appear in the obvious place, look elsewhere.

(14 August 1993)

Directories and Place Names

One early problem every genealogist faces is finding the exact location of a relative's home. This knowledge is necessary for deciding which other documents to use. In an earlier column we explained how to use local directories to find this information.

How do we find the directories themselves? A publication of the National Library of Canada, *Canadian Directories 1790-1987: a Bibliography*, by Mary E. Bond may do the trick. Ask for it at your local library.

Bond lists 1200 directories covering 21,500 places across Canada. Most directories include more than one place. Bond lists the places by their current name. If your ancestors lived in Smithville, you will want to look in the section for Wellesley village. If you are not sure of the name changes of your ancestral village over the years, consult Floreen Carter's interesting *Place Names of Ontario* (1985). It charts the differences.

Bond's list includes volumes in the collections of the National Library and National Archives in Ottawa only. Locally held directories will be missed, so be sure to enquire in libraries in the area which interests you as well.

The introduction to the bibliography is a good one, describing the purpose of these directories and many of their peculiarities. Genealogists eager for family information often ignore the introductions in texts they consult. It can be worthwhile to find out what the experts have to say. Bond gives us a great deal to consider.

Not everyone made it into the directories. People were missed by not being at home when the enumerator called or refusing information. Some people were left out by design. A.B. Cherrier, compiler of a Quebec directory during the 1880s, wrote, "Names of residents in houses of ill fame are not inscribed in the Street Key."

Although the directories listed are available in Ottawa, those published before 1900 are also on microfiche put out by the Canadian Institute for Historical Microreproduction (CIHM). A complete set of their publications can be seen at the University of Waterloo library.

(21 August 1993)

Update: Floreen Carter's Place Names of Ontario *went out of print quickly, but can still be purchased in microfiche from Information Graphics, Box 1843, London N6A 5H9. This is the most useful place names publication for genealogists.*

Tax Records

Every year we receive a tax bill. So did our ancestors. They were probably no happier to see theirs than we are. They had extras on their tax bill too. They were assessed a certain number of days' work to keep the roads in order or do other manual labour. We are only expected to pay money, not time.

The records of these annual taxes, called assessment records, can be valuable to researchers who want to know when their ancestors lived in a certain area and how long they stayed there. Other land records tell us only about owners of property, but assessment records include tenants as well.

Each of our local municipalities has assessment records for most of this century. About twenty years' worth of Kitchener's are missing, thrown out at the time the new city hall was built in 1924. Wilmot's early records had an adventurous time in the top of a barn for many years, but now are well kept at the Baden library.

The nineteenth century records for most of the townships were missing or survived only spottily. Our careful ancestors had made a second copy of each, however, which were stored in the basement of the county courthouse. The historical good sense of regional chairman Ken Seiling came to the fore in 1986, when he had these old records microfilmed. They can now be consulted at the Kitchener library. This is a good example of "lost" records being found and made available through the generosity of those in charge.

How are they useful? Since they are annual and include everyone, look at them year by year. Your ancestor will appear as soon as he comes to town. When he disappears, you know he has moved on. Most of the records are arranged by letter of the alphabet. All the "A's" are together, all the "B's" and so on, although not in strict order. It is a quick business to trace any family. As usual with records from a century ago, only the husband is listed. If a woman is listed, she is a widow or spinster.

The exact address is also given, and sometimes the man's age. This is an unusual (and undependable) source to find a person's birth year. The age is only as correct as the person who gave it to the township clerk. We have no way of knowing who that might have been.

As researchers have to do more work in twentieth century records, assessments will come into their own. We often lose people as they move around, but assessment records are a big help. Although modern records are usually listed by address rather than name, they can be used in conjunction with city directories and telephone books.

The most current assessment records can be found at the city or township hall. Older records may have been moved to an archives or library. Kitchener sends its assessments to the public library. Old ones for Cambridge are at the municipal archives.

This week's question comes from Dona Madill of Cambridge, who has an ancestor named Thomas Park. In the 1851 and 1861 census' she finds him listed as born in Ireland. She recently received a letter from a woman who found a Thomas Park born in Fredericksburgh, Ontario. The correspondent thinks they are the same person.

Dona suspects they have two different people. I think she is right. Without knowing what facts point to Fredericksburgh, we do have contemporary documents (the census) which state that Dona's Thomas was born in Ireland. Even three of his children were born there (also from the census).

Because the census is a document created at a time when the person may have given the information themselves, it must be treated very seriously. The more contemporary the document, the more force it has as genealogical evidence.

(4 September 1993)

Using Maps and Atlases

The most neglected part of genealogical work is geography.

Everyone who undertakes to do family history in any area should make themselves familiar with the terrain. Once you find your ancestors' house or farm, get a map and colour in the lot so it stands out.

Using your other resources, find the church they attended, their cemeteries, post office and the homes of relatives. If you mark all these on the map, a pattern will emerge, showing you the 'community' in which they lived. Now you can see that the roads, rivers and railway lines in that area had some effect on how your ancestors' lived. With slower transportation, they had a more restricted scope for movement.

If you have had trouble discovering what churches or cemeteries your family used a century ago, looking at old maps will help you. The best possibilities are the series of historical atlases first published in the 1870s and republished in the 1970s. These contained township maps, many with names of lot-owners included, brief histories and engravings of illustrious residents. These people paid to have their faces and houses included in the book.

The reprint series of these atlases are readily available in most libraries. There are volumes for most counties in southern Ontario.

The township maps include railway lines, churches, schools and mills. The latter may be of help to you too. Every farm had to take its grain to the mill for chopping into feed. The store near the mill might have had your family's business. The accounts of either the mill or the store might still exist in an archives or a local historian's collection. If your family had a page in the accounts, you will learn a great deal about their way of life.

If the lot-owners are indicated near your family, study the names. Do you see ones you recognize? You probably do, for people tended to intermarry with their neighbours' families.

In the 1890s my grandmother was a girl on her father's farm. Up and down the road within two miles lived six uncles, an aunt and a great-uncle. Three of those brothers lived side by side, yet each had a different postal address. They had chosen different villages for their shopping and so picked up their mail at different post offices.

If you trace the route of a river, you will see how it affected the way roads were built. The placing of bridges made a way across, but by the same token, no bridge meant no communication between the two banks of the river. Look at the way the roads are cut off or veer south and north in Woolwich township for an example of this. If your family lived near a river, it affected their way of life.

Once the railway arrived, travel between some villages was quick and easy, changing peoples' lives. Some residents might remember when the train ran between Elmira and Galt, stopping at rural places such as St Jacobs and Doon along the way. With a dozen trains a day, people could pop into Kitchener for some shopping, which was very different from being isolated in the country.

Studying maps can be useful, and you should always have one of your ancestral area on hand for consultation. Most counties have map offices. The Region of Waterloo sells regional maps in pocket or wall sizes. They are available at the regional planning receptoinist's desk on Frederick Street. If you want to call them to discuss it, telephone 575-4533.
(11 September 1993)

Nineteenth Century Weddings

In the past people often did not marry where we expected them to.

We might think that people would go to their local church and have a 'traditional' wedding. The bride marched down the aisle and all her friends watched from the pews. In fact, only a few couples married this way.

Large weddings of this kind were often held at home. Some people married in church, but not many could afford the expense. For the majority, a quiet wedding in the manse or the clergyman's study was the best alternative.

In pioneer days, couples waited for the circuit rider to come by and were married then.

Some churches had rules about who could be married by the minister. Both bride and groom had to be members of the church, for instance. If they were not, or the parents had some objection, the couple had no place to turn.

Luckily, most places had a Marrying Sam who would perform the ceremony for anyone who came along. In this area, it was F.W. Bindemann, founder of many of the oldest Lutheran churches in Waterloo County. People came for miles to be married at his house in Greenbush, the forest between Kitchener and Waterloo. (It was located on land now occupied by the Central Meat Market parking lot.)

Once the railway arrived, there was another possibility. Couples who wanted to marry would board the train, travel to a nearby town and seek out a sympathetic clergyman. They might stay overnight in a hotel or with friends, but the trip would be short one.

This quiet means of marrying ensured it would be cheap and easy. Perhaps there would be a small celebration with friends once they reached home, but no big bills for fancy clothes or catering.

Genealogists looking for marriages performed between 1860 and 1940 would do well to consider these "railway marriages" as a possibility, if you cannot find the information in the home town. My own grandparents were married in Peterborough, a town twenty miles from where the family lived. One of my aunts, married in 1933, travelled from Bowmanville to Belleville to be wed, stayed overnight with her cousin and returned home. She still says, "We left home with two dollars and we came home with two dollars."

To find the place, look at an old map of the area, and trace the railway lines. Look for the next sizable place, one where people did not often go. For instance, from New Hamburg I would look toward Stratford rather than Kitchener.

(18 September 1993)

Waterloo County Churches

Finding the records of individual churches may be more difficult than you think. Flood, fire, unthinking custodians and mice have all contributed to the loss of old documents. Sometimes the records will not have been kept at all.

For people looking for old church records in Waterloo Region, the job is now considerably easier. The local branch of the Ontario Genealogical Society has published *Waterloo County Churches: A Research Guide to Churches Established Before 1900*, by Rosemary Willard Ambrose.

Mrs Ambrose began her research as part of a province-wide inventory of 19th century church records. Her own dedication and the rich resources of Waterloo Region led to the publication of this 275-page book.

For each congregation, she includes a brief history, a summary of the records and their location, and the church's address. There are photographs of most of the buildings as well.

The usefulness of this information will be obvious to seasoned researchers, who know that details of our ancestors may not be in the first church we come to. Being able to trace the development of our denomination through the short histories of various congregations may help us find records which would otherwise elude us.

For instance, a family from St Peter's Lutheran Church in Kitchener looking for an ancestor's marriage in 1855 will find that their congregation had not been founded yet. They will look instead at the records for St Paul's in Kitchener or St John's in Waterloo.

One of the troublesome questions in church history is the date any congregation started. Do we use the first meeting, the formal incorporation of the parish, the date of the building's erection? Mrs Ambrose has been particularly meticulous in establishing just when each congregation began. Her work in various church archives and ancient yearbooks and newspapers will help many churches clarify their own histories.

This book will be a standard reference work in this region for decades to come. Every local genealogist will want to have one. The bargain price is $27.00. The book is available at OGS meetings or from the University of Waterloo bookstore and Words Worth Books.
(25 September 19930

The Archives of Ontario

Last week's announcement of the newly available Vital Statistics records may leave many genealogists considering a trip to the Archives of Ontario. I urge you to pay them a visit.

As the official repository for Ontario government records, the AO has an astonishing number of documents. They have all the census records, including those census-assessments we discussed some weeks ago, which predate the every name census' begun in 1851.

Before civil registration began, there were other forms of marriage registration in the form of county and district marriage books, some of which go back to the 1830s and 1840s.

Although most of the original wills are now in a warehouse in Mississauga, they have been microfilmed and are in self-service drawers in the AO reading room. These cover wills from 1792 to about 1960 for most counties.

The Ontario Genealogical Society has produced transcriptions of the gravestones in many of the cemeteries in the province. Copies of these booklets are on microfilm.

One of the greatest collections of documents are the series' of materials on land transactions. These include copies of the original grants to the first settlers in the province, discussions of Loyalist claims, and the millions of sales of lots which have occurred since. If you think that your ancestor had an original grant, consult the Land Grant Index at the Kitchener library before venturing to Toronto.

In the series called Township Papers are miscellaneous records which have come to the Archives over the years, arranged by lot and concession under the township's name. Once you know where your ancestor lived, have a look through these papers and see if any of their documents happened to survive.

Aside from the traditional genealogical documents, you may want to look at some of the other government records which are kept at the AO. Court records, for example, remind us of long-ago cases in which our ancestors may have been involved. Not long ago, I enquired at the Alberta provincial archives about a bigamy case of 1939 which interested us. The reply included original documents, including a letter from the bigamist to his second wife, asking for a reconciliation. Similar files may be found in Toronto which might interest you.

The most used materials are on microfilm, much of it self-service, but a great many of the collections remain in their original old and fragile forms. Diaries, correspondence and family papers can be located using the various card indexes or finding aids in the reading room. Begin any visit by asking for a tour and explanation which will help you get started.

Those planning a visit to AO should telephone them on their toll-free line (800-668-9933) and ask for a brochure on using the reading room. Ensure that the day you are planning to visit is not a Social Contract closing day.

If you go, you will find the archives at 77 Grenville Street, Toronto, in the Queen's Park area. Parking is available in the Elizabeth Street garage across from Toronto Hospital, two blocks south of the archives. If you want to avoid heavy parking fees, leave your car elsewhere and come on the subway, getting off at College. The archives is two blocks away.

The reading room at the archives is comfortable and quiet. To obtain a pass, you will need to have identification with your address on it with you. Remember, they do not allow pens in the reading room, so bring a good pencil and don't forget your glasses! You will be asked to leave your belongings in the cloakroom or a locker, bringing only essential notes inside.

There are two desks at the doorway, one for general information and the other to advise genealogists. The archivists are helpful and understanding, but cannot do research for you. Bring your questions and come well prepared, for the wealth of material will astonish you.
(9 October 1993)

Preparing For Overseas Trips

The big leap for genealogists means crossing the ocean and beginning research in Europe. In Oktoberfest week, it seems appropriate to look at records in Germany.

You must know the town or village your ancestors came from. You may find the name in a document here if your family has not passed down some version of the name. Death certificates, gravestones, church burial records, newspaper obituaries are a few of the sources which may list the elusive birthplace.

I was once asked by a journalist (not from this newspaper) where his family came from. He was leaving a few days later for Alsace and wanted to "do his family tree." There was no time for the proper research. He flew to France and looked up his name in the telephone directory. Finding a few people with his name, he proceeded to knock on their doors and ask if they were cousins of his. They did not know and he wrote an angry account of their lack of family knowledge when he returned.

While telephone books can be useful resources at other times, they are not useful if you are hunting for a home town. Do the searching in Canada first.

Once you have found your German village, have a look at Angus Baxter's *In Search of Your German Roots* to determine how to proceed. You might also look at *The Atlantic Bridge to Germany*, a multivolume set of guides to Germany church records, which lists availability parish by parish in the old West Germany. (East German volumes are in preparation.) Both of these titles are available at the Kitchener library.

You will want to write to the village even if you are planning a visit. Write two letters. Send one to the mayor, asking for information about the town. The other should go to the clergyman, who has charge of those valuable church records.

If your German is not good enough for letter writing, look around you. Kitchener-Waterloo has many German speakers who might be willing to help you. Ask at the friendly German clubs for assistance. For the technical genealogical letter to the clergyman, go to the information services desk at the Kitchener library. They have a file of sample German genealogical letters. All you have to do is fill in the blanks with your family names and dates, and send the letter off.

Canadian church records are kept chronologically, as each event happens. In Germany, old records were kept by family, each page devoted to one name. Thus, two or three generations of your family might be found in a single location, making the search so much easier.

If you decide to visit, be sure to arrange your appointment with the local clergy well in advance. They are busy men and may not be home when you call unexpectedly. Avoid disappointment by writing ahead, stating exactly what you will be looking for. You may find they will have done the search before you arrive, leaving you to copy the information and chat with them about local customs.

I know of many local people who have paid visits to their ancestral villages and found distant cousins still occupying the family home. They are warmly welcomed and hear the full story of the house, farm or family business. The clergy or mayor will know if anyone who might be a cousin still lives there. If there is a local historian or genealogist, be sure to pay them a visit too. They will know everyone in town and all the stories--perhaps including yours.

If your family came from the former East Germany, you will find records and resources less easy to locate. The value of the tourist dollar means they will still welcome you, so don't be shy.
(16 October 1993)
Update: The East German volumes of The Atlantic Bridge to Germany *are now available. They should be available from local libraries*

Adoptees Search for their Birth Parents

Adoptees start out knowing less about their blood relations than the rest of us. I always say they are lucky, however: they belong to twice as many families as we do.

For many adoptees, the need to know about the circumstances of their birth is a pressing one. A part of themselves seems missing. My colleague on a nearby page of this newspaper, Ann Landers, feels strongly that no good can come of searching for birth parents, but I disagree. From helping numbers of people in their searches over the past decade, I have realized that the need to know overcomes other considerations.

Since adoption records conceal the birth name of the child and the parents, people begin the search with a handicap. They may literally know nothing. If you are an adoptee who wants to begin your search, I have three suggestions.

First, get in touch with the Adoption Disclosure Register, which is part of the provincial government in Toronto. You can telephone them at (416) 327-4730. They will send you a form on which you can register your wish to contact your birth parent or child. Your name will be on file, and should your birth parent also register, you will be put in touch with one another.

I also suggest that you visit the Children's Aid Society or other agency who handled your adoption. While it may be easy to telephone or write to them, I suggest a personal visit (make an appointment ahead). They can examine your file, give you the non-identifying information about your parents which the law provides and perhaps make a suggestion about what to do next.

In the past, social workers in these agencies have been reluctant to disclose anything about birth parents or adopted children. Those attitudes have changed. They now realize how much you have a need to know.

I have been told that these agencies sometimes put a priority on finding parents if the adoptees are now over fifty years old. There is an urgency about finding elderly parents.

Thirdly, try to see if your family connections can tell you anything. Your own parents may know the birth mother's name, may even have met her. If your adoption was treated with shame or secrecy in the family, now may be a time to clear the air.

I have known those who were afraid to ask their parents about the adoption because no one had ever discussed it before. Approach them in a calm and loving way. Tell them how much it means to you and be sure to reassure them that anything you find will not change your love for them. Caring for you as they do, they will be able to answer your questions.

If your parents are no longer living, ask aunts, cousins or close friends of theirs if they know anything. They may have helped your parents in your first days at home and be privy to information about the adoption.

If you are lucky enough to find a parent, grandparent or sibling, be prepared for anything. The emotional urgency you feel may not be shared. You may be welcome, but you may be rejected.. A strong relationship is unlikely. Whatever happens the adoptee should view it as a growing experience.

In the cases I have seen, the birth families most often feel a great sense of relief at being found. The sad circumstances of years before are often forgotten in the pleasure of seeing a happy, grown-up child.

Once you have some information to work with, keep in mind that libraries are gold mines of information for this kind of search, using city directories, old telephone books and high school yearbooks.

(23 October 1993)

Update: a useful new tool for those looking for people whose exact location is unknown is the PhoneDisc. This is a CD-ROM publication listing every-one in a given area in alphabetical order. There are also Internet websites with the same function, such as Canada 411. Ask your reference librarian for suggestions about these resources.

Death Cards

Among the treasures found among the keepsakes of many families are printed cards which announce a death. These are valuable and reliable sources of information.

Death cards come in two formats, folded or flat. The flat ones may be printed on paper but are more likely stiffened with cardboard. For a time there was a fashion for dark green or black paper with gold writing, which was suitably gloomy.

The folded ones are more common. On the outside will be words such as "In Memoriam" or "Thy Will Be Done". Inside are the details of who died, when and where, their age and, in the case of a woman or child, some relationship. Opposite are instructions on how to get to the funeral, which would be held from the home of a family member.

These cards had two functions. They announced the death and served as an invitation to the funeral. Nearby friends could be sent a copy for delivery in the next day's mail. The growth of education meant that most people could read a little so these printed invitations were appropriate. Faraway relations would appreciate the notice too.

The cards also served as memorials to the deceased. Death cards of family members would be kept forever, as a reminder of when they had passed away.

In towns, the cards were soon visible in store windows. Many places had only a weekly newspaper and needed somewhere to announce funerals more quickly. Copies of the cards were placed in store windows. Passing shoppers would stop to see who had died.

Later, funeral homes might have a small box fixed at eye level on the main street, with the cards of their current clients prominently displayed. I saw one of these still in use in Georgetown in 1990.

The habit of displaying death cards in store windows went on for many decades. Jimmy Patterson, longtime hardware merchant in Ayr, kept the cards he took out of his window in a drawer of his desk. Over five decades he had quite a collection, a record of Ayr people in the twentieth century.

In the 1920s and later, these cards sometimes indicate the funeral is "private". The public invitation common on death cards had begun to attract those who attended funerals for entertainment and the free food which followed. Private funerals were meant to discourage these freeloaders.

The use of these cards died out after World War II, when people began to use the daily newspaper as their best means of announcing a death. Many people continued to have them printed, however, and some funeral homes made up a handful as keepsakes for their clients.

If we find these cards for members of our own family what can they tell us? The reliable information will be the date and place of death, and the place of burial. If a relationship with someone else is given, it is trustworthy too. Unfortunately, ages on death cards may not be accurate. Use them as a guide rather than a fact.

The relationships given on death cards are usually for children and women. In the patriarchal past, a man's name could stand on its own. A child would belong to its father; the mother's name would also appear in more recent cards. Husbands were listed on their wife's cards. The form "Relict of James Lunn" was common, "relict" being a more formal word for widow.

These death cards have now become collector's items, both as family mementoes and for those interested in Victoriana. Archives often collect death cards for their area of interest. Photocopies of the cards in Jimmy Patterson's collection (which has now disappeared) can be seen at the Kitchener library. (30 October 1993)

Patronymics and Family Nicknames

Everyone in Canada has an English-style name now, but their ancestors may have named themselves in quite different ways. Many countries used patronymics instead of family names. Here, the father's name was used to describe the person, in a form which would read in English 'son of —'.

This was especially true in Scandinavia and has resulted in names such as Lars Larsen, Jakob Knudsen or Eric Jonasson. At some point the patronymic changed into a firm family name. Eric's ancestor named Jonas may now be several generations back.

Names in this format are common in Norway, Sweden, Denmark, Iceland and even parts of Finland. One guide says that names ending in -son are Swedish (or possibly Norwegian), names in -sen are Norwegian or Danish and names in -sson are Icelandic or Norwegian. (However, I have a Swedish niece named Andersson.)

I am pleased to say that there are also feminine forms in Norway and Iceland, indicating 'daughter of —'. The heroine of a great Norwegian saga is Kristin Lavransdatter and the current president of Iceland is Vigdis Finnboga-dottir.

Patronymics are still used in Iceland. I am told that the telephone book there lists people by their first names because of this.

Certainly, the huge indexes of the Latter-day Saints family history centres had to deal with this situation by listing people in these countries by their given names. It would be pointless to list people by their patronymic if no one knew what it was.

In Wales the most common surnames today are based on the patronymics which were used there for so many years. These include Jones and Johns (from John), Morgan, Lewis, Davidson and Matthews. The Welsh used the word 'ap' (son of) in the form Morgan ap Rhys (Morgan son of Rhys). They would string these together in miniature genealogies, Morgan ap Rhys ap Llewellyn ap Morgan.

The Russians still give a patronymic which is used as a middle name, the male form ending in -vich (son of) and the female in -ovna (daughter of). The last Tsar was Nicholas Alexandrovich (son of Alexander), his sister was Olga Alexandrovna. Even in casual conversation, these long forms were used, which is what makes reading Russian novels so confusing. It does make genealogical research easier, however, to have a hint what the father's name is.

Sometimes names change for political reasons. When Italy took over the Adriatic islands of Croatia in the 1930s, the Croatians had to change their names to Italian forms. After World War II, they changed back, but documents from the occupation period will be in the unfamiliar form.

On the island of Susak, there were only eight family names. With a tradition of naming each first-born son after his paternal grandfather, there were many who had the same name. To differentiate among them, each family had a nickname. These nicknames were used more frequently than the formal names.

Antonia Bussanich became Antonia Bussani in the Italian period, but her family nickname was Franecova. The nickname was in fact a matronymic, taken from her mother's father's first name. Because of the frequent use of 'Antonia' in her family, she was known familiarly as Toncili. When she revisited Susak in the 1980s, she would introduce herself as Toncili Franecova for easy identification. In Canada, she is known as Toni.

Any genealogist working in an area where names have changed or nicknames are common should be on the lookout for unusual ways of identifying their ancestors in the documents they examine.
(13 November)

Anglican Records in Ontario

Records from the Anglican church are of particular importance for family research. In the early days, everyone had to be married by an Anglican priest, so even those of Methodist or Presbyterian background will want to know where the Anglican records are. The "Only Anglican Marriages" rule ended in 1832.

Because Anglican clergy were used to marrying anyone who came and asked, those in need of a wedding knew where to go, even in later days.

There are eight dioceses in the geographical province of Ontario, each of which have their own rules about their records. Adding to the confusion is that there is a geographical province, an ecclesiastical province and a diocese, all called Ontario and none the same. We know the geographical province, of course.

The ecclesiastical province of Ontario consists of everything we know geographically except a slice of the North-West, which is part of the diocese of Keewatin. Keewatin is in the ecclesiastical province of Rupert's Land and its records are in Winnipeg.

The diocese of Ontario is based in Kingston and consists of an area of south-central Ontario on the lake (also called Ontario).

Details of the archival holdings of the other seven diocese are contained in a book with the breathtaking title *Guide to the Holdings of the Archives of the Ecclesiastical Province of Ontario* (1990).

The dioceses of Ottawa, Ontario and Niagara (based in Hamilton) all have canonical laws requiring that old parish records be deposited in their archives. Ottawa and Ontario have their own diocese archives, details of which are contained in the *Guide*. The diocese of Niagara keeps their records in the Mills Library at McMaster University. They require a letter of permission from the parish priest before you look at the old records.

The diocese of Algoma is based in Sault Ste Marie and Moosonee is in Schumacher. Although there is a small archives in Schumacher, many of the Moosonee records are on microfilm at the General Synod archives in Toronto. Since these two dioceses are in the north, their records tend to be more scattered than those in the south.

The two largest dioceses are Toronto and Huron (based in London). Toronto has made an effort to collect their materials at their archives, but much remains to be done. The archivists there are very helpful in trying to determine which records exist for churches who have not sent anything into the central repository.

The diocese of Huron, in which we are located, keeps its archives at Huron College in the University of Western Ontario. There has never been an emphasis on archives in the diocese, perhaps because no bishop has taken much of an interest. Most churches keep their records in the vestry or the rectory.

If the *Guide* does not list the parish whose records you need, look at the *Anglican Year Book*, which will give you the address of the current parish priest. Write to him with a simple request and you might receive an answer. If your local library does not have a copy of the yearbook, your local Anglican church will.

Many Anglican records begin in 1858, when new books were provided. If you are seeking records before that, ensure that there was a resident priest in the area which interests you. In early days, there may only have been a travelling missionary. Berlin's earliest Anglican priest came from Milton. His circuit covered eleven townships north to Egremont which took three months to ride through forest and mud. His records have not been found.
(20 November 1993)

Update: Records of the Diocese of Algoma are now located at their new archives at Laurentian University in Sudbury.

Methodist Records in Ontario

The largest religious group in Canada today is the United Church. It began as a group of smaller churches in the nineteenth century, principally the various Methodists. Many of us have Methodist ancestry because they were the only church in town.

Methodism grew out of the Church of England in the eighteenth century. John and Charles Wesley preached a new and simpler religion hoping to revive the state church. Their followers became so abundant they eventually formed a denomination of their own. At the beginning of the nineteenth century, renegade Methodist preachers began their own congregations if they had differing theological views with the main church.

Both mainstream Methodism (called Wesleyanism) and the breakoff groups came to Ontario in its early days. In the early census columns under "Religion" you will find entries which say merely "Methodist" but most will give you the name of the particular sect. There were Primitive Methodists, New Connexion Methodists, Episcopal Methodists, Bible Christians and, the largest, Wesleyans. These are often shortened in the census entries to their initials (P. Meth., N.C. Meth., B.C.)

Because Methodism had evangelism as its base, there was a tradition of circuit-riding missionaries throughout the province. Small churches were established even in remote villages. Tiny country churches sprang up at crossroads without any houses around them. They served the farming community in the vicinity.

The farmers in a given area would be glad to have their own church nearby, however small it was. They might also find themselves in disagreement with their neighbours or the local preacher on some theological point and begin a new congregation. The result was a proliferation of these little log cabin churches dotted on back concessions.

The Primitive Methodists based one of their circuits in Drayton and Arthur, with many congregations throughout Peel township. There were so many Primitive and other Methodist churches in Peel, we cannot name them all any more. Evidence tells us that in the 1860s, there were about twenty-four Methodist churches on the nineteen concessions of Peel.

Most of these churches have left little evidence beyond a line in an annual report of the time or mention in a newspaper account of evangelistic meetings. One, in the country near Alma, is now a farmer's field. The only sign that a church and its cemetery were once there is a single gravestone propped against the fence.

Eventually all these various groups began to join together once again. By 1884 the smaller sects had come together with the Wesleyans to form the Methodist church.

In 1907 the Congregationalists joined them. They were an independent group whose history went back to the dawn of Protestantism. If your family was Congregational before 1907, you should look at Douglas Warkentin's unpublished history of the sect, available at the United Church Archives.

In 1925 the majority of Presbyterian churches came together with the Methodists to form the United Church of Canada. The few Methodist churches which stayed out of the union were known as Free Methodists. One of their churches remained in Galt.

Because each Methodist congregation was independent and self-governing, they were responsible for their own records. This often meant that records were not kept in an orderly way or were lost. Fires at the church, manse or secretary's house damaged many more.

To find Methodist records, enquire at the church itself or at the United Church Archives, which is in the University of Toronto (75 Queen's Park Crescent East, Toronto M5S 1K7). When there were so many small churches in a district, you may find it difficult to tell which your ancestors belonged to.

In our area, the majority of Methodist churches seemed to spring up in the period 1840-1870. Their early records consist of marriages and baptisms often beginning about 1865. Burials were kept later.

The Wesleyans recognized the importance of baptismal records and kept a central registry of baptisms which antedates the records of many individual congregations. Microfilm copies of this registry for the whole province are available locally at the Kitchener public library. Norma Huber prepared an index to the entries for Waterloo and Wellington counties, also at KPL. It is wise to check the surrounding counties when looking for your ancestors in the Wesleyan records, keeping in mind those far-reaching circuit riders.

(4 December 1993)

Scotland

Family research in Scotland is quite different from England. Although there were fewer people, many of them bore the same handful of names, and anyway the records are not as complete .

The Scots resisted the idea of parish record keeping. Although the earliest kirk book records the marriage of Mary, Queen of Scots to Lord Damley in 1565, most records do not begin until the eighteenth century. They have all been gathered into the Scottish Record Office in Edinburgh.

At the Latter-day Saints family history centers, you will find one large index to all the pre-1855 Church of Scotland registers. Because people moved about so much, and so many had the same names, this big index was created to help genealogists sort out the confusion.

Please remember if you do not find your ancestor in the Ancient Parish Registers index that it is for Church of Scotland records only. This means official Presbyterianism. There were many break-off groups, known as non-conformists, as well as the Episcopal Church of Scotland (or Anglicans). Their records are not in the index, although many of them are also at the Scottish Record Office.

Civil registration in Scotland began in 1855 and the documents are much more informative than the English or Canadian ones. Be sure to consult the certificates even if you know the date of your ancestor's event. You might find something very useful has been included. Certificates and information can be had from the Registrar General for Scotland, New Register House, Edinburgh EH1 3YT.

Perhaps the most difficult part of Scottish genealogy is dealing with so many people who have the same names. We all know unhappy genealogists searching among the thousands of Margaret MacDonalds or Robert Robertsons.

A common habit when christening babies was to follow the Scottish Naming Pattern. The following was often done:

the eldest son was named for the father's father
the second son was named for the mother's father
the third son was named for the father
the fourth son was named for the father's eldest brother
the fifth son was named for the mother's eldest brother

and so on. It applied to girls too:

the eldest daughter was named for the mother's mother
the second daughter was named for the father's mother
the third daughter was named for the mother
the fourth daughter was named for the mother's eldest sister
the fifth daughter was named for the father's eldest sister

If names would be duplicated, you simply skipped to the next name in the series.

The result was a great many people but only a few names. It makes Scottish genealogy rather complex. You should also be careful of names which have been anglicised. MacHamish, for instance, was changed to Jamieson.

If you visit Edinburgh, you will want to visit New Register House and the Scottish Record Office. Lorna Ferguson, who had such a profitable time in Edinburgh this past summer, says the ladies at the Scottish genealogical society were very helpful.

If you cannot make the trip, begin by looking at Gerald Hamilton-Edwards' *In Search of Scottish Ancestry* (2d ed., 1983) or Alwyn James' *Scottish Roots*. Then see if you can find your ancestors through the LDS family history center.

You may find you do not need to take that Scottish holiday, although I bet you will still want to.

(11 December 1993)

Update: A new book on Scottish research may be more timely for researchers today. Sherry Irvine's Your Scottish Ancestry *(1997) is available from SEL Enterprises, Bos 92, Thornhill L3T 3N1. Irvine is an authority on British research.*

Telephone Directories

If you are searching for lost twentieth century people, old telephone directories can be useful.

We are all familiar with the form of the telephone book. People are listed alphabetically by name or initial. Nowadays, most households have a phone, but that has only been true since the affluent fifties. Before the Second World War, many homes did not have one, so they will not be listed.

The first telephone books were published in the 1880s for Ontario. There were so few subscribers that the slim booklets covered all of south-western Ontario at first. Gradually the books became bigger and the area covered smaller. The *Record*'s distribution area is now covered primarily by three books, one for Kitchener-Waterloo-Guelph-Cambridge, one for Stratford and one for Owen Sound.

You can discover where people lived using telephone directories, not only the town but the street address. Having placed people in a certain town, you can use other documents—city directories, church records, cemetery files —to find out more. In an early column, I mentioned that you must know three things to start a genealogical search: a name, a place and a time period. Directories can be useful to firm up your knowledge of the place involved.

If you are looking for old telephone books, please do not go to the phone company office, as they cannot help you. The Bell Telephone Archives in Montreal has made microfiche copies of old phone books available locally in each location served. The K-W-Guelph books are available at the Guelph library and the Owen Sound books at its public library. Stratford books are at the Stratford Public Library. The Kitchener library has an incomplete set of original local volumes.

If you are looking farther afield, a complete set of the Ontario fiche can be found at the National Library in Ottawa or the Metro Toronto Reference Library at Yonge and Bloor in Toronto. If you are looking outside Ontario, write to the Bell Archives for assistance. They are located at 1050 Beaver Hall Hill, Bureau 820, Montreal, Quebec H2Z 1S4.
(18 December 1993)

Divorce Records in Canada

Divorce nowadays is a common occurrence. In the past it was less frequent and more difficult.

Prior to the 1960s, divorce was handled through a private act of the Parliament of Canada. Each one had to be treated individually by the legislators in Ottawa. The time taken and expense should be obvious.

Garnet Richmond of Kitchener has asked how he can find the particulars of a divorce which may have taken place in the early 1920s. Accessing these early divorces may actually be easier than later ones, which would require a search of court records.

I always advocate looking at every document possible. If you have a divorced member of your family from this early period, be sure to examine the private act for their divorce. It will contain useful information.

Finding the dates for these short-lived marriages in the past may be difficult, as no one remembers the unhappy occasion now. The copy of the act will contain this date and perhaps more which you will find useful.

Because each divorce was an act of parliament, it is necessary to go through the indexes to the federal statutes. These can be found in any large library with an extensive government documents section, such as the University of Waterloo.

If the divorce you are looking for occurred between 1867 and 1916, look in the Index to Private Acts 1867-1916. Look under both names to be sure you have not missed the one you want. You will find a reference to the year and chapter you need.

For divorces after 1916, there is no convenient cumulative index. You must check each annual index. Perhaps a family member can help you estimate what year the divorce took place. If not, it is a simple matter to search through many years of the index.

****

Paul Gross of Kitchener has found a way to discover where elusive **Roman Catholic records are in Europe.**

He needed access to the records of his grandfather's home village in Poland. During the long Communist occupation, it was almost impossible to find these registers, and they may be anywhere now.

After a consultation with his parish priest, Paul wrote to the papal pro-nuncio in Ottawa. This is the pope's ambassador to Canada.

The nuncio passed his request on to the Bishop of Krakow, who found the records. Not only was Paul put in touch with the parish priest in his grandfather's village, he found some of his long lost cousins there, too.

Paul sent a letter of introduction from his parish priest when writing to Ottawa, but I think that diplomatic courtesy will ensure that anyone writing will receive a reply. If you want to discuss the matter with the papal pro-nuncio, write to H.E. the Most Rev. Carlos Curis, 724 Manor Ave., Rockcliffe Park ON K1M 0E3.

Please keep in mind that correspondence with European countries should be sent in their own language when possible. If you have to write in Polish, Hungarian or Croatian but your knowledge of these languages is less than literary, look around you. We live in a multicultural community and one of your neighbours will be glad to help. There are also various ethnic clubs who have friendly members. To locate a club or church of the language you require, ask the Kitchener library's Infolink at 743-7502.

(8 January 1994)

Writing Narrative Family Histories

Most people panic when the time comes to actually write their family history. You have lots to work with. You should not be afraid.

Many completed genealogies consist only of pages of names, with birth, death and marriage dates attached. While this represents a lot of work, it is not fun to read. It will only be used as a reference tool for future family discussions.

If you want to write a family history which will be read, you must include some narrative sections. The easy way to do this is to write short biographies for some members of the family and insert them in appropriate places. They are less difficult than you think.

First, include the birth, death and marriage dates, plus the places where each happened. Flesh out the times between with details and stories.

Was she named after someone? Find out why. Someone I know was named for her second cousin's fiancee, who had been one of the midwife's assistants at her birth.

A physical description is good: short or tall, fair or dark, glasses, strong hands, a loud laugh. Perhaps bright blue eyes run in the family. My own are blue, but not as bright as my father's. He liked to remember his own grandfather's, spread out on a table in the living room. He had lost an eye in an industrial accident and the eye salesman came by occasionally to sell him a new one, which had to match the other exactly.

What did he do for a living? This can often open new vistas to modern readers, who have no idea how our ancestors lived. The blacksmith, the harness-maker, the cobbler have all largely disappeared from our world. Many of my female ancestors were glovers. They sewed gloves together from forms brought to their homes, then picked up when finished.

Describe where they lived. If the house is still standing, descendants may want to visit.

If they were active in their church or school board, mention it. Some details of their work there may be found in old records.

Perhaps a family legend or document will give you some information about an experience or event which must be included. The most common of these is the story of how the emigrant family came across the ocean.

The cause of their death, and its circumstances, will always be of interest. The release of the nineteenth century Vital Statistics records recently in Ontario has opened many doors, one of them being knowledge of the cause of our ancestors' deaths.

Finally, include information about where they were buried and if there is a gravestone. If it has in interesting inscription, write it down. Cousins reading on a cold winter night will be happy to know the details.

I urge everyone to write these brief stories, even if you are not actively pursuing other genealogical goals. Later generations will thank you.

Best of all, include some anecdotes which will reveal the character. When I asked about my grandmother's grandmother, three of her grandchildren said the same thing. "Her eyes were not supposed to be very good, but watch out! She had an eye in the back of her head that could see whatever you did!" It summed up my ancestor Louisa better than anything else.
(15 January 1994)

Brothers with the Same Birthday

This past week I celebrated the thirtieth anniversary of my start in genealogy. I thought I had heard all the problems, but was humbled by a letter from Allan McCullough of Waterloo. He presented me with a unique difficulty.

Allan's grandfather's bible states that he was born on 22 September 1867. However, his grandfather's brother also claimed to be born on that day, and the two men were not twins. Their tombstones give both men the same birthday. How can we find the truth?

First, let me say that tombstones are a bad witness to anyone's birthday. They are created long after the birthdate itself, and in fact when the person involved is already dead. The source of the information might be anyone.

What we need to find is a contemporary document which gives the birthdate.

If you can determine the religion of the family using the census, try to find a baptismal record for each. It will state the birthdate.

Since baptismal records can be hard to find, an easier way is to use the census. Look in the 1871 census, which has been indexed for all of Ontario. In the family's listing, the little boys will have their ages given, and you can determine their approximate birthdates.

If you would like an exact day, look at the 1901 census, when everyone had to give their exact birthday as well as age. If I were Allan, I would look at the census for both years.

The 1871 census index is available at the Kitchener public library, as is the census itself for Waterloo, Wellington, Perth and Huron counties. If the one you need is elsewhere in Ontario, visit Wilfrid Laurier University library.
(5 February 1994)

Update: Some weeks later, a letter from Allan told me that he had sorted out his problem and discovered why the brothers seemed to have the same birthdate. One was, of course, a year older than the other.

Post Office Householder Directories

Looking for lost modern relations can be difficult. In an earlier column, I discussed commercial directories and telephone books. Recently, I found another resource at the National Library which is invaluable.

Commercial directories cover only large cities across the country. Smaller towns and rural areas cannot be accessed in this way.

From 1964 to 1977 the post office tried to remedy this problem by publishing the Post Office Householder Directories. These provided lists of heads of households in every area of Canada not covered by the commercial directories, including the rural routes of the big cities.

The books were produced as a service to business. They were also made available in an "automated format" (which in those days meant punched data processing cards or magnetic tape) and address labels.

There is a volume of the Householder Directories for each federal riding in Canada which is not contained in a commercial directory. In 1968, there were 144 volumes.

Inside, the names are listed alphabetically under each post office. The first names must contain no more than four letters, so most people are listed by initial. If the name is given, it is shortened. For instance, "Harold" appears as "Haro."

The mailing address of the time is given. Occupations are given, in coded form. This may help to sort out people of similar names.

Potential users should keep in mind that only "householders" are listed. This usually means the senior male present. People who lived with relations or boarded are not included. Robert Lovelock and his family, who lived at RR #1, Napanee, are not listed. Their household can be found under the name of his father-in-law, W. Raycraft, who lived in the same house.

For those who are looking for a lost relation in this period, these books are very useful. They are simple to use, if you know the name of the federal riding. In most cases, it is a place name. Several ridings may be found in a volume.

The books can also be used by those searching for birth parents. For these people, the lack of rural directories has always been very trying, but these Householder Directories solve the problem. They were published during a time period in which many current adoptees seeking birth parents were born.

Unfortunately only one set of these volumes seems to exist in Canada. It is at the National Library in Ottawa. Even the post office did not keep copies.

A number of other libraries have selected volumes, probably for their local area. The National Library, 395 Wellington Street, Ottawa K1A 0N4, will be happy to answer queries about the books, including referring you to other libraries which have the volumes you require. Because the National Library has only one copy of each volume, it may not be possible to make these items available on interlibrary loan. Of course, they can be consulted in person if you go to Ottawa.

If you want to see if a nearby library has copies, the National Library suggests checking the UTLAS database for locations. This database is available at the University of Waterloo library.
(12 February 1994)

Alsace

Many of our local families came from the Alsace region on the French-German border. Because of the good documentation here, researchers find themselves able to pay a visit there to look for ancestors.

Alsace now consists of the two French departments called Upper Rhine (Haut-Rhin) and Lower Rhine (Bas-Rhin). Many of the families there were originally Swiss Mennonites, who moved to Alsace for religious reasons.

Lorraine Roth of Waterloo has done extensive work in Amish records both in our region and Alsace. She advises that you should know the name and birthdate of the person you are going to research, plus their town or village of origin. There are many sources here in Canada which will yield the village name if you do not know it already.

A listing of those who left the province can be found at the Latter-day Saints family history centres, on six rolls of microfilm entitled the Alsace Emigration Index. Unfortunately, Miss Roth tells us it is not as useful in the period 1820-1837, which is when many people came to Waterloo county.

You should also consult the Ancestry File at the LDS family history centre. It is wise to take an early look at the Ancestry File no matter what country interests you.

In France, you will want to look at the civil registration records (Etat-Civil). These begin in 1792, during the French Revolution. Previous to 1792, you will want to consult the parish records.

The Etat-Civil records may be found in the town hall (Mairie) in the place where your ancestors lived. The official event would have been recorded here. Even now, in France, there must be a civil wedding as well as the religious ceremony.

There may also be records in the state archives for each department. For Bas-Rhin, the address is 9 rue Fischart, 67200 Strasbourg. For Haut-Rhin, write to Cité Administrative, 3 rue Fleischauer, 68000 Colmar.

Researchers used to the meagre details in many Canadian official records will be pleasantly surprised by the thoroughness of the French. Birth records include mother's maiden name and the ages of the parents. Marriage records include the bride's and groom's mothers' maiden names and even the ages of the witnesses. Be sure to make a note of everything, even if you do not think it useful right away. It may be vital later.

Records in the period 1792-1804 are given in the Revolutionary Calendar used in France during that time. If you find events in the form "17 Brumaire, Year 8", bring them home with you. At the Kitchener Public Library reference department, you can consult *The Book of Calendars*, which will translate these back to our own form.

Whether visiting the state archives, mairie or parish church, please remember that you should have an appointment and the hours of opening may not be as extensive as you would wish. Be flexible enough to fit in with French customs.

Many of the parish registers you will need to look at have already been microfilmed and are available through the LDS family history centre from Salt Lake City. Keep this in mind when pursuing researches in your limited time abroad.

You should also be sure always to write in French to Alsace. If you are unsure how to phrase your needs, ask at the LDS family history centre to see if they have any sample letters. If not, write to the European Reference Department, Genealogy Department, 50 East North Temple, Salt Lake City, Utah 84150 USA. They have samples available.
(19 February 1994)

National Service Census, 1940

In many countries, every individual carries identification papers which may be produced at any time. There is already discussion of a Canadian National Identity Card, complete with fingerprints.

In the past, our government had no way of naming or tracing individuals until the establishment of the Social Insurance Card in the 1960s. The exception was the 1940 National Registration.

To help determine what labour power was available at the beginning of World War II, the government asked everyone to fill in a form describing their background and abilities. These records are now housed by Statistics Canada in Ottawa. Since they include information about birthplace and parentage given by the people themselves, their usefulness to genealogists should be obvious.

Since these records are of fairly recent date, they are still considering private. Their availability is determined by the Access to Information Act.

If you want to obtain the record of a member of your family, you should obtain an Access to Information Request Form from your local public library or directly from Statistics Canada. It will ask the name of the person and birthdate (if known) and place of residence in 1940. If the latter is a problem, you should use city directories or telephone books to find your missing person.

There is a fee of $5.00 per request. You must also supply proof of date of death of the person. Although StatsCan prefers a copy of the death certificate, a newspaper obituary will do. The person must have been dead for twenty years or more for the information to be available. You may not access records of living persons.

Once you have a response, you will find that you learn a great deal about your relative.

Of course not everyone filled out the form. Some people would have been missed and those living in institutions (including Ontario County Houses of Industry), members of religious orders and the armed forces were excluded.

Poles in Wilno: Reta Lapointe of Kitchener writes: I am interested in finding all I can of my ancestors who were of Polish descent & settled in a small village called Wilno, Ontario. They were to have landed in Norfolk Virginia in 1864. The original Polish church burned down many years ago.

The loss of the church records is a problem, but your ancestors came to Canada at an early period. Since you know they lived in Wilno, you should begin by consulting the census, which will give you an idea of their birthdates.

If they were in Ontario by 1871, you are in luck, for that census is indexed for the whole province. Be sure to look carefully, for Polish names would almost certainly be misspelled by the English-speaking census taker.

The 1901 census is also good, because it gives exact birthdates and the year immigrants came to Canada. Both these census' for Wilno are at Wilfrid Laurier University library.

If you want to look at the ships' passenger lists and immigration records in Norfolk, Virginia, you might find the name of their ancestral village in Poland. Consult the guide to US National Archives records at the Kitchener public library about how these work. The nearest place to find them is the Allen County Public Library in Fort Wayne, Indiana (just one day's leisurely drive from here).

If you begin working in Poland, there are several guides to help you. The newest is *Korzenie Polskie/Polish Roots*, by Rosemary A. Chorzempa (1993).

(26 February 1994)

The Civil Service List
and Causes of Death

If you had a relative who worked for the federal civil service in the first decades of Canadian life, you might be lucky.

The bureaucracy was large even then, so to keep track of who held what job, the government published The Civil Service List. It was sometimes called The Blue Book of the Province of Canada.

It gave details on who held what jobs in the civil service, when they were appointed, their previous work experience and salary. Some editions also included the person's date of birth.

The series starts with Confederation in 1867 and goes up to 1918. There are volumes for most, but not all, years.

While the date of birth is the only one of the basic genealogical facts found in this source, it can be used for other family tree purposes. Having the details of the person's employment record can add an interesting paragraph to your narrative family history. Since the books were published over a fifty year period, it can be possible to follow one man's entire working life.

I use the word "man" in the previous sentence carefully, for there were few women in the civil service in this period. In the later volumes, dealing with the early twentieth century, some women would have occupied positions as secretaries or typists. These persons were called "typewriters" in those days.

Although we might think of the civil service being strictly in Ottawa, in fact even a century ago there were federal employees all over the country. The listings for the post office, railway and fisheries department show this clearly.

In the 1887 edition, there is one listing in the customs and revenue department for Berlin (Kitchener). Anson Lewis Bowman was customs collector here. He was appointed 8 April 1880 and earned $900 a year.

The only other customs employees in Waterloo County were Thomas Peck and William Alfred Dennis of Galt. Peck had been appointed in 1884 and earned $800. Dennis was a new appointment in 1887 and earned $500. These were lucrative positions in those days as well as being steady and long-lasting.

The lists are set up in a way that makes finding an individual easy, but most are also indexed.

These books are available in the government publications section of the National Library in Ottawa. Many of them are on display in the reference room, for easy access.

The union catalogue at the National Library indicates that few of these Civil Service Lists are available elsewhere in Canada. Because of their rarity, it is possible that they may not be sent out on interlibrary loan. However, the staff at the National Library will be glad to help you with any questions you might have. In addition, the prospect of fifty years of these volumes may be another incentive to make a genealogical trip to Ottawa.

You can reach the National Library by writing to 395 Wellington Street, Ottawa K1A 0N4.

Causes of death: An Ontario Genealogical Society newsletter editor recently observed that, after looking at the newly available death certificates at the Archives of Ontario, she had only learned about a great-grandfather's cause of death.

Since the great-grandfather in question died in 1877, the information would have been lost had she not found it in the certificate. We have such an interest in our family's medical history nowadays, that learning an ancient cause of death should not be termed "only." It is a new fact of great significance.

As well, examining these certificates provides us with confirmation of information from a primary source. The fact that the information on the certificate does not contradict anything we have learned previously should be an accomplishment in itself.

When you approach archival documents, try to keep a positive attitude, not seeing the minimum, but the maximum that they can tell you.
(5 March 1994)

Irish Church Records

Genealogists face difficulties in Ireland. For once, the Roman Catholics are luckier than the protestants in their search for records.

At the turn of this century, the government of Ireland decided to gather the Church of Ireland (Anglican) records into a central archives. They were in danger from mould, fire and mice in their many country churches.

The process of gathering them took a couple of decades. By the time it was over, the Troubles had begun. One of the terrorist acts which preceded Irish independence in 1922 was the burning of the central archives. All the gathered records were lost.

As church records are the basis for most genealogical searching, Irish searchers have to work around this problem.

James G. Ryan is a genealogist with his own publishing company, Flyleaf Press near Dublin. His massive guide, *Irish Records And Sources For Family and Local History* (1988) is a good place to start.

The book is divided by county, with plenty of maps for guidance. He assumes you know where your family came from. The geographical side of genealogy is so important. In Ireland, you should know the parish or village, and then find out the townland and barony if possible, for many records are organized this way. Also keep in mind that for the Republic of Ireland, there were county names under the British regime which have now changed. Be aware of both forms for later use.

The counties are divided by parish and the other geographical peculiarities of Ireland (townlands, baronies) are explained. He describes what is left of the census, which also suffered in the fire.

Parish by parish, he lists what he knows about the records. For the Roman Catholic parishes, the addresses are given, so that you can contact the parish priest for assistance. Everyone I know who has dealt with them has found them helpful.

The best genealogical handbooks provide plenty of addresses, and Ryan's is no exception. He tells you how to get in touch with newspapers, libraries, research services and family history societies.

Ryan's new book is *Irish Church Records* (1992). He has asked experts in the field of each denomination to describe the situation with their records. There are separate chapters on Roman Catholic, Church of Ireland, Quaker, Huguenot, Jewish, Methodist, Presbyterian and Baptist records. The last three are of particular importance in Ulster (Northern Ireland).

This is less a parish-by-parish handbook than a general introduction to the subject, which everyone should read before the plunge into the intricacies of the records themselves. This is true if you are a beginner or a veteran, for there are always new things to learn.

In fact, the genealogical profile in Ireland has changed considerably over the last several years. Because they face the lack of certain archives which other countries take for granted, the Irish genealogical community is working to reconstitute what records they can. The advent of the computer has meant that many tiny resources can be brought together in the form of databases to help new researchers. These databases are often in county or city record offices. A number have been begun using youth employment projects to establish the early entries.

James Ryan's *Irish Records* is available at the Kitchener library, and we hope his *Irish Church Records* will be there soon, too. If you would like a leaflet describing his many Irish genealogical publications, write to Flyleaf Press at 4 Spencer Villas, Glenageary, Co. Dublin, Ireland, enclosing a long self addressed envelope and three International Reply Coupons. Flyleaf Press Books are available in Canada through SEL Enterprises, 178 Grandview Avenue, Thornhill ON L3T 1J1.
(19 March 1994)

Criminal Indictment Files at Archives of Ontario

Really lucky genealogists have a criminal in their background.

Back in the days when family historians looked for glory and blue blood, this was not true. Now, the top Australian families are those who descended from the earliest convicts. The rest of us have to make do with lesser felons, but the results are the same. If you have a criminal in the family, your research is easier.

As research in court and jail records becomes less complex, it is always wise to take some time to look over the indexes for the area which interests you. If a family name pops up, have a look to see if some useful information is included.

One of these good resources are the Criminal Indictment Case Files at the Archives of Ontario in Toronto (RG22 Series 392). These are the initial papers dealing with criminal indictments and date from about 1860 to 1930 or so. The finding aids are particularly useful. The materials are organized by county, with indexes alphabetically by charge and a separate listing for female defendants.

The files are relatively small, often with only the charge sheet and a deposition or two. Sometimes there are surprising additions.

One case in 1894 details a charge of rape against Henry Oppertsheiser. The event took place on his farm, lot 78 GCT in Woolwich, a detailed map of which is included in the file showing the location of all the buildings. The purpose of this was to determine if Mrs Oppertsheiser, in the house, could have heard if the young girl involved had screamed in the barn.

An interesting sidelight of this case is a petition, signed by 250 men of Woolwich including the reeve, asking for leniency for Oppertsheiser because he had a young family and "had suffered enough."

An 1895 file deals with a charge of murder against Auguste Kruschinski. The body was found on his farm, near the corner where Kossuth Road meets what is now Fountain Street (the Breslau-Preston road). This file also includes a map, showing the neighbouring farms with names attached: Hagey, Schiedel, Sauder, Wenger, Detweiler.

An interesting case of 1882 charged Charles Lowell of Galt with inciting perjury. An innkeeper, Lowell was said to have made Janet Craig McEwan pregnant. He was charged with paying McEwan $75 to lay the blame at the door of George Houck instead.

The indictment uses many flowery phrases in the style of old-fashioned legal documents, but its description of Lowell should not be missed. It says he was, "a person of an evil and wicked mind and disposition and not having the fear of God before his eyes."

We do not know what happened in these cases, because only the indictments are included. To follow the case further, you would have to look at the trial records, which is another matter.

If you want to examine the Criminal Indictment Case Files in search of those valuable and felonious ancestors, you will have to pay a visit to the

Archives of Ontario, 77 Grenville Street in Toronto, as the files are not on microfilm yet. Ask the archivist on duty for assistance.

Genealogists in pursuit of the obvious records and dates might be tempted to forego the work involved in looking at archives such as these, which are off the beaten track.

My own work with some jail records in Great Yarmouth, England made the difference between success and failure. Attracted by one volume of the records which was on display, I asked to see more. From the index I learned that my great-great-great-great uncle, Payne Hewitt, had been jailed in 1851 for beating his wife and again later for not providing her with the necessities of life.

His jail records provided me with a physical description of this unknown relation, a short, mousy-haired man with piggy eyes. But it also told me his birthplace, far away across the county. From there, it was a short trip to looking at the church records for the birthplace, where I found a long list of baptisms for Payne and his siblings.

Criminal ancestors really do pay off.

(26 March 1994)

United Empire Loyalists

When the American Revolutionary war ended in 1783, those who remained loyal to King George had to leave the 13 colonies. Many returned to England or went to the Caribbean, but a significant number came to Canada. They are now known as the United Empire Loyalists.

The earliest Loyalists came in 1784. The king was so touched by their devotion that he gave these emigrants the right to put UE after their names. This right continues with their descendants today. The United Empire Loyalists' Association of Canada promotes the study of this group and assists its members to trace their ancestry back to approved UE settlers.

To celebrate the bicentenary of the first Loyalist settlements in Ontario, the Toronto branch of the UEL Association published *Loyalist Lineages of Canada* (1984), a three-volume set of genealogies. Even if you are not sure about your family, it is worth checking the index to find out if they appear there.

The difficulties faced by potential UEL members are great. Most people can trace their Canadian families back to about 1850, using the usual census', church records and civil registrations. Before that, searching becomes

62

more difficult. Tracing all the way back to UE ancestors in the 1790s can be onerous.

One of the principal problems is establishing who is or is not UE. Many people in the mid-nineteenth century claimed to be the children or grandchildren of Loyalists, but these were merely early Ontario settlers. They might even have been "Late Loyalists", people who came in the 1790s, but they are not really Loyalists at all.

Loyalists and their children were eligible for grants of land. This encouraged their loyalty but also helped to settle the new colony. The records which detail the claims for grants and the evidence provided form a wealth of genealogical information for UE researchers.

The 1904 report of the Archives of Ontario tried to detail the Loyalist land records which they owned. This book has been a basic tool for Loyalist research ever since. Despite its age, it is generally available in libraries. It was reprinted in 1993 by Genealogical Publishing in Baltimore, Maryland, in two handsome volumes. You should have no trouble finding it in some version.

A couple of decades ago, some new UE land claims turned up in London, England and New York State. These were the missing volumes which would have been included in 1904 had they been identified.

The Archives of Ontario published the new evidence in 1985 with a collation of all the UE evidence by Bruce Antliffe. This interesting project included a cloth-bound book with the new material, a microfiche reprint of the 1904 report and a folio of drawings and maps on the subject. This bicentennial set is available at the Kitchener library and many other locations. The book is entitled *Loyalist Settlements 1783-1789*.

The local UEL association is called the Grand River Branch. It serves the Grand river watershed. Its aims are to bring together UE descendants, preserve the history of Loyalist families and collect new UE materials.

It publishes a newsletter twice a year. Members also receive the national magazine, the *Loyalist Gazette*.

Meetings are held on the 3rd Sunday of the month. Information about the UEL Association can be obtained from them at 50 Baldwin St., Toronto M5T 1L4; telephone 416-591-1783. Local information on Grand River Branch can be had from Doris Lemon, 349 Craigleith , Waterloo N2L 3B5.
(2 April 1994)

Ontario's Jail Registers

Two weeks ago I made a passing reference to jail records in my discussion of criminal ancestors.

Jail registers in Ontario are archival police records, now stored at the Archives of Ontario, 77 Grenville Street, Toronto. There is a century-long rule of secrecy for these records, so you can only look at cases from 1893 and earlier.

This is curious, because the Criminal Indictment files go up to about 1930. It is possible to examine the indictments, but one may not then go on to see what the sentence may have been.

There is one jail register for each county in Ontario. Case records indicate the charge, the sentence and the criminal's residence and religion. There is little personal information included, unlike the English jail records which I mentioned.

The records are not indexed, but are chronological. It is a simple matter to find the material you want if searching for a particular name. Those doing historical work on certain types of charges will also find the searching simple.

As well as the usual burglary and assault charges which are the staple of jail records everywhere, you will find a great deal of vagrancy and prostitution.

Vagrancy is especially common in the winter, when wanderers who could be happy in the countryside during the summer came to town to get warm. If they lingered too long, the long arm of the law would put them in jail for a day or two before sending them on their way. People from out of town were particularly unwelcome. In 1876, the Waterloo County Gaol (gaol being the old word for jail) was host to Louis Hoffman of Philadelphia on a vagrancy charge.

The Windsor records (held at the Windsor Municipal Archives) record a great many elderly women who make return visits to the jail as vagrants. Perhaps the police there were very keen on cleaning up their city. As in our own day, the homeless had no place to go in the winter. While there are charitable shelters for the homeless now, in the nineteenth century the rules were more strict. For example, the shelter for homeless women in Hamilton would take only those who came recommended as being respectable by a ranking member of society.

Not many of the wandering poor knew ranking members of society.

If you visit the Archives of Ontario, you will find the jail records in RG20 F19. The holdings are detailed in Finding Aid 20. An archivist will help you find what you want. If you really need to see a case from 1894 or later, you can apply to see it to the archivist in charge of court records, detailing the reasons you need to see it. If he agrees, you will be able to examine the records only if you agree not to publish anything about them.

Waterloo County court books held at the Archives of Ontario include a police court Minute Book for Galt 1857-1920, a supreme court Judgement Book 1881-1909 and a Masters' Docketbook 1897-1930. Because these are court rather than police records, they are available for public scrutiny.

Jail records may be difficult to use but they do give us a sidelight on our ancestors which is available nowhere else.

Lingelbach Cemetery: George Robb of Milverton asks about the records of this little cemetery, which can be seen on highway 8 between New Hamburg and Shakespeare. Its church faces it across the road.

A transcription of the stones in Lingelbach cemetery can be found at the Stratford-Perth Archives (24 St Andrew St, Stratford N5A 1A3). The archivists there will know who is responsible for the cemetery and hence hold the records. There may not be a cemetery record for 1887, when Mr Robb's great-grandfather died, but there might be a church burial record.

Another alternative for finding grandad's death is the civil registration records in Toronto. The index is available at the Latter-day Saints family history centre in Kitchener. Check there first.
(9 April 1994)

World War One Soldiers

Do you have a soldier in the family? Few Canadian families can answer, "No," to this question. The Canadians who volunteered to serve in the two world wars came from every part of the country and most families.

The most informative genealogical information about soldiers comes from their individual files. These records tell us where and when the man (or woman) enlisted, their date and place of birth, family members (either next of kin or wife and children) and details of their service careers.

These details can be interesting in themselves. Those who served in battle will have their on and off line experience given, wounds, illnesses, leaves and any other activities that might have provoked comment from officers.

My great-uncle, Harry Taylor, had an uneventful time in this army until he was killed at Ypres in Belgium in the fall of 1916. His service record runs to only a few pages (some have dozens). He enlisted at Swan River, Manitoba, giving the name of his brother Arthur as next of kin. They had no memory of ever seeing one another, although they had last met fifteen years earlier.

Harry had a sore foot once he got to England. In June 1916 he was hospitalized with pneumonia for a week before returning to the front lines in France.

We know almost nothing about my great-uncle, so the service record is a valuable glimpse into his life.

Harry was put in the orphanage when he was six years old, three weeks after the drowning death of his father. He came to Canada at the age of 13 with many other child emigrants.

As a result, he lock track of his birthdate and, surprising to us, his name. He was known simply as Harry, although he had been given the grand moniker of Henry Robert Hewitt Taylor in the slum where he was born.

At the time of his enlistment, Harry must have felt that he needed a bit more of a name than the one he owned, so he christened himself Charles Henry Taylor for the benefit of the army. When he died, this was the name on his official papers and on his gravestone in the military cemetery in France.

His brother named a son Charles Henry after Harry, never knowing the truth about the name. And that little boy was delighted to discover the name "Charles Henry Taylor" on the war memorial in Oshawa, their home town. This did not refer to Uncle Harry, but little Charlie claimed that it was, because it meant he got an extra day off school every 11 November to attend the cenotaph ceremonies.

Soldiers' personal records are government by the Freedom of Information Act, but in 1992 the government of Canada declared the records of World War I soldiers to be in the public domain. If you wish to access the story of any individual who fought in the war, you have only to ask.

If you want to add a colourful page to your family history, send whatever details you have about your soldier to the Personnel Records Centre, National Archives of Canada, 395 Wellington Street, Ottawa K1A 0N3. Expect to wait a while for the reply, as they are swamped with requests.

Keep in mind that these records do contain some hard genealogical data as well as the military background information. Researching the father of a cousin, I was able to find out the names of his children from a first marriage because they were listed, along with their mother, on the form when he enlisted in 1915. Their ages had been erased, for reasons of their own privacy. (30 April 1994)

World War One Unit Diaries

Last week, I talked about individual soldiers' records from World War I, the ones which Glenn Wright has said describe, "every aspect of a soldier's life and activity from enlistment to demobilization." There are many other kinds of records which will also be worth examining if you have a military ancestor.

War diaries were kept by all units in the field. From your relation's personal record, you will be able to determine what unit he joined. You can read the unit's actual diaries from the battles they fought or their times off the line in England or France.

While you might find your relation mentioned, often the officers are the only ones whose names are included. However, others might appear if they had acted in a particularly brave or unusual fashion.

Depending on your view of the war, you should be prepared for some matter of fact descriptions of the most harrowing events. I spend a week before Christmas of 1978 reading the war diaries of the 9th Royal Ulster Rifles for the first battle of the Somme in 1916. On 1 July of that year (12 July in the old Julian calendar, and still known as "The Black Twelfth" in Belfast), 800 soldiers made an early morning attack on the German lines. There were extraordinary feats of bravery. The colonel commanding the regiment, Frank Crozier, ended the day with his uniform torn by bullets in several places, but without a wound. Less than 80 of the grave Ulstermen returned. There were so few, the regiment had to be disbanded.

Each unit will also have a file giving details of its life in the military. They will describe the official view of what happened to the various regiments and brigades.

You may remember the scenes in "Gone With the Wind" when the civilians gathered at the newspaper office to read the casualty lists as they came off the press. It was the quickest way to learn who had been wounded. These lists were also compiled by the Canadian government during World War I. Enquire about these various records at the National Archives of Canada, 395 Wellington Street, Ottawa K1A 0N3.

If your soldier died, his gave is cared for by the Commonwealth War Graves Commission, which has an Ottawa office. They will be able to give you the exact location of the grave and details of its care. The government of France ceded the land occupied by the cemeteries to the British Empire in 1915.

If your relation belonged to the Royal Flying Corps or the infant Royal Canadian Air Force, his personnel files will be gone. However, they have a card index describing each airman as best they can. This file can be seen at the Directorate of History, Department of National Defence in Ottawa. Navy files are also scanty, but they have casualty lists, also at the Directorate of History.

If your relative won a gallantry medal while fighting with the Canadian forces in World War I, he will be listed in a new series of books published by Kirkby-Malton Press (Box 24027, 1853 Grant Avenue, Winnipeg MB R3N 2B1). David Riddle and Donald Mitchell have compiled lists of those receiving the Distinguished Service Order ($19.00); the Military Cross ($29.00); the Distinguished Conduct Medal ($27.00), a total of 5999 awards. Given the social structure of the time, these will have gone almost exclusively to officers. You should be able to find these books in the reference section of your local library.

If you have a connection with a winner of the Victoria Cross, the highest award for courage in the British Empire, you will find his story in a number of books listed in your library's catalogue under "Victoria Cross."

(7 May 1994)

The Canada Gazette

Data which will help researchers turn up in the funniest places. Few of us would want to wade through a pile of government publications, but it can be rewarding.

An old copy of the *Canada Gazette* turned up at a garage sale. A sharp-eyed genealogist found that it was packed with things for researchers. More experienced researchers know that the *Canada Gazette* can be found at most large libraries in the periodicals or government documents sections. In our area, look at the Kitchener, University of Waterloo or University of Guelph libraries.

The *Canada Gazette* is the official organ of the federal government. They use it to make announcements or place statements which are legally required. It is not easy reading, but can be helpful to those looking for information about bankruptcies, changes of citizenship and, in the old days, divorces. There is also a provincial equivalent, the Ontario Gazette

Perhaps the greatest interest most people have in these publications is the listing, each spring, of deserted bank accounts looking to be claimed. The Ontario volume also contains listings of land confiscated for non-payment of taxes, which will be sold cheaply by the Sheriff.

However, these are not the genealogist's delight. In the days when divorces had to be passed by an act of Parliament, they were announced in the *Canada Gazette*. If you need details on a divorce from the distant past, you will still find it there, but you must know the date of the decree to start looking.

If you had a relation who was bankrupt, you can find notices under the Bankruptcy Act which names the debtor, their residence and the date of the bankruptcy.

Military announcements often occupy a great deal of space. Shifts in command, promotions and decorations all became official once they had appeared in the *Gazette*.

The genealogical bloodhound who turned up her single copy of the *Canada Gazette* in a British Columbia garage sale said it was dated 1936. It contained a 24 page listing of aliens who had recently been naturalized by the Secretary of State.

As well as the list of aliens, another section listed aliens with children (who automatically became citizens when their parents did). The children are listed. There were also lists for those who were reclaiming their Canadian citizenship, were becoming citizens with their husbands or who were being granted citizenship after their background as British subjects had been in doubt. Occasionally, someone's citizenship was revoked, and notice of this was also in the *Gazette*. These lists could be of great interest to researchers, but the difficulties of looking through years of lists might deter the less hardy.

(21 May 1994)

Methodist Episcopal Baptisms
& Schleswig Holstein

Many of the early Methodist churches have no records. Either the congregation did not keep record books or they have been lost.

The more evangelical the congregation, the less chance that there were records kept in the early days. With ministers travelling from town to town, it was often no one's job to keep track of the events in the church. When something is no one's job, no one does it.

The lack of registers makes genealogical searching harder. As we know, the Wesleyan Methodists had their ministers send in an annual report of the baptisms they had performed. These were transcribed into a ledger in Toronto, and these records may be the only evidence of a birth we can now find.

There were other branches of Methodism at work in Ontario around 1850. One of these, the Methodist Episcopal church, was quite small in numbers. However, the officials of this church seem to have picked up on the Wesleyans' good idea. They had a central registry of baptisms for their Niagara conference. This ledger, unpaged and difficult to use, has now been indexed.

The Niagara conference covered a large part of southwestern and central Ontario, from Howard and Goderich in the west to Orono and Whitby in the east. Entries for Toronto in the central ledger seem to be scanty, but there are plenty for the countryside, about eight thousand in all.

Louise Hope, a former president of the Ontario Genealogical Society, has indexed and published the details of all the baptisms. She notes in her introduction that using the original ledger is difficult, so she copied out all the information given there except for the name of the officiating clergyman. Because she knew that researchers would want to check the original, a type-written copy of the ledger has been left at the United Church Archives in Toronto. The published index is alphabetical.

Information included in the index is the name of the baby, its birth and baptismal dates, parents and birthplace. Unfortunately, the maiden name of the mother does not seem to have been recorded.

You may know from your census searches that your ancestors were Methodist Episcopal. Even if you are unsure, there is always a chance they took their babies to the nearest Methodist church of whatever kind for baptism, and checking this index will not take long. Make a point of having a look at it.

Index to Niagara Conference Methodist Episcopal Church Baptismal Register 1849-1886 is published in two volumes by the Ontario Genealogical Society (102 - 40 Orchard View Blvd., Toronto M4R 1B9). The price is $15.00.

Schleswig-Holstein Roots: Most of the early German settlers here came from southwest Germany (Alsace, Hessen, Baden). There were always those who made their way here from the east. We find pioneer names from Prussia, Pomerania, and Mecklenberg. A few came from the Danish border, Schleswig-Holstein, including the Ahrens family. Carl Ahrens was an early Berlin clerk and many will remember the Ahrens shoe factory on Queen street across from the Walper Hotel.

An interesting difficulty of genealogical research in Schleswig is that people often changed their family name. If they bought a farm whose name was different from their own, they would begin using the farm's name. If you cannot document these changes, you might find it impossible to tell who your family is.

If your family has connections in Schleswig-Holstein, you might like to see the newsletter of the American/Schleswig-Holstein Heritage Society. Its purpose is to preserve the heritage of those provinces and encouraging cultural exchanges, and to sponsor family history research. The meetings may be too far away to attend, as they are held in Davenport, Iowa. However, the newsletter is crammed with information and maps which will interest you.

Since these two provinces have both Danish and German heritage, there is material of use to those from Denmark. For instance, a new Danish Immigration Museum has opened in Elk Horn, Iowa, and Queen Margrethe has agreed to be the patron. Elk Horn lies on Interstate 80 between Omaha and Des Moines.

Among the society's publications is a cookbook, a local map and a small book on *The Frisians in Schleswig-Holstein* ($4.50 postpaid). For more information about the society write to ASHHS, Box 313, Davenport IA 52805-0313 USA.

(23 July 1994)

Canadian Railway Records

As we all know, Canada was a country built on the railway. Pierre Berton told us so.

Now, the railway is dying, but many of our families were employed by the companies that laid the iron tracks. Before 1916, there were over a thousand documented railway companies across Canada. Their records might contain a gold mine for some researcher.

Althea Douglas and her husband, Creighton Douglas, have gathered the information on these records into an informative book, *Canadian Railway Records: A Guide for Genealogists*, published recently by the Ontario Genealogical Society. It will be of particular interest in places such as Stratford, a town which owed its prosperity to the railway in the days before the theatre was built.

Mrs Douglas gives us good advice about where to go. She tells of seeing Clark's *History of the Early Railways in Nova Scotia*, which had "seniority lists" from 1925 of engineers, firemen and trainmen. Naturally, this book will not be available locally, but remember that interlibrary loan will bring a copy from the National Library or elsewhere. This history is one of many railway histories.

Aside from information about the records themselves, the Douglas' provide us with a quick history of life as a railway employee. In the days when there were ten or so trains a day running between Galt and Elmira (via Doon, Kitchener and Waterloo), there were many people involved and they were busy. In the small stations, "the agent was jack-of-many-trades. He was telegraph operator, sold tickets, received and delivered express and freight, collected and remitted money." The railway station was in many ways a centre of the village, competing with the post office for the honour. Times have changed.

Records of many smaller companies which became part of the Canadian National Railways are at the National Archives in Ottawa. A detailed list is contained in the book.

The Canadian Pacific archives is at Windsor Station in Montreal. Using this facility for genealogical work is not as simple as Ottawa, but as Mrs Douglas says, Enjoy Montreal! The personnel records are also at Windsor Station, but in a different department. They seem to be inaccessible at the moment.

The Douglas' then travel across the country looking at local railways and record repositories which hold their archives. There are so many that they cannot list them all, but give a representative sampling. The canny researcher can use these examples to ferret out the rest.

Nearby repositories listed include the Archives of Ontario in Toronto and the Hamilton Public Library (which holds the Great Western Railway archives 1845-1882). The University of Western Ontario library in London cares for the Grand Trunk Railway materials, including time and wage books 1903-1919.

The book ends with an extensive bibliography indicating where other information on railways can be found.

Most Canadian families will have at least one member who worked for a railway. This book will be useful for genealogists who want to pursue that person. It is available for a bargain price, $8.50 (plus postage and GST), from the Ontario Genealogical Society, 102 - 40 Orchard View Blvd., Toronto M4R 1B9.

(6 August 1994)

Software Puts Photos on Disk

Pictures are one of the big problems in producing family histories. Most genealogies are produced in small numbers by photocopying. They have dark or smudged photos.

I have seen laser reproductions of old photographs that are almost as good as the originals. They are often in sepia tones which have a period feel. The cost of the reproduction is prohibitive on a large scale, however.

Bette Schmadl of Kitchener told me recently of her Wilhelm family history, stored on disk to be printed when needed. She has 200 photographs covering a century of history, but they have to be stored separately in paper copy.

A new and inexpensive computer program can solve this problem. It provides a way to save and print photographs using your PC and home printer.

As well as creating a new way to illustrate your family tree, it provides a new means of document storage. When a friend demonstrated this new software to me, he had a collection of gravestone photographs on disk which he displayed on his office monitor. The stones could all be read clearly and the colours were just as they were in the cemetery.

In addition, someone with sophisticated camera equipment could photograph old documents (including church records, wills or letters), which

73

could then be reproduced on paper almost in their original condition. For the first time, we can present evidence in the form that we find it in an archives.

The system is called PhotoWorks/Pictures on Disk. You do not need a CD-ROM drive or any other expensive equipment. It works with any IBM-compatible PC with 640k of RAM and a high-density 1.44 Mb 3 1/2 inch or 1.2 Mb 5 1/4 inch floppy disk drive. It can also be used with an Apple Macintosh with a software that allows you to run DOS applications, such as SoftPC. There are plans for a Macintosh version of Pictures on Disk in the coming months. There will also be a version for Microsoft Windows.

Installing PhotoWorks is simple. Even I managed to follow the instructions and I am no expert.

Needless to say, this is not merely a genealogical tool, but meant for anyone who wants to save pictures in a compact and easily transported manner.

The company which deals with Pictures on Disk is Seattle FilmWorks, but it has a Canadian outlet and price list. For $11.95, you can have 24 pictures transferred to disk. The software to run them comes with your order.

When you have a 35mm film processed (24 exposrures), you can have another set of the photos on disk for $4.95. For 36 exposure film, the cost is $6.95.

What this means is that you can take a series of new pictures for use in your family history or have those staid Victorian ancestors reprocessed. The process works with both prints and slides.

The software enables you to catalog the photographs as well. You can name and describe each picture, then check through your collection when you set up a printing or showing.

The pictures can be printed easily, for use in letters if you wish. You can send copies via modem, or make copies on disk for mailing to family members.

Seattle FilmWorks recommends the software not only to genealogists but also for real estate salespeople and writers. For the editors of small newsletters (churches or genealogical societies, for example), it seems to me to be a step into a new and glamorous world. It must be the wave of the future.

You can write to Seattle FilmWorks at Box 94598, Richmond BC V6Y 2V6. They will send you a brochure about PhotoWorks.

If you want to get started right away and see how it works, you can send the 24 pictures (regular size prints or slides), plus US$11.95 and shipping costs. They accept VISA and MasterCard.   (20 August 1994)

Update: The new digital cameras, which first appeared in 1996, are able to provide pictures which can be downloaded directly into your computer from the camera. Although early models are very expensive, their price is dropping monthly. In addition to the photos on disk, you can also have your pictures on-line. For $10.30, Seattle FilmWorks will send a message to your e-mail address with a code word. Using it at their website, you can download your photographs directly to your hard drive. Write to them for details.

Basic English Genealogical Handbooks

A recent letter asked me if I would devote a column to basic handbooks on English research. I have not done so before, but that was an oversight.

There are a number of good basic books on England (aside from Scotland, Ireland and Wales, each of which is different).

The one you are most likely to find in Canadian libraries is *In Search of Your British and Irish Roots*, by Angus Baxter. This book was published in 1982 and consequently is getting a little old, but it is helpful. Baxter is an Anglo-Canadian, so he has first-hand experience in using the English sources and also a Canadian perspective. He begins with some introductory material on general records, but most of the book is a county-by-county listing of addresses and parishes. The parish listings are inadequate, giving only the geographic name and no dates or details.

The data on record offices has changed considerably, as many of them which previously refused to do research for mail inquirers have now set up money-making offices to do just that. This is very good for those of us who want some small thing examined but are not sure who to hire to do it. The county employees who run the record office enquiry services are bound to be trustworthy.

Anthony Camp's *Everyone Has Roots* (1978) is also old and likely to be found in libraries. Camp is the director of the Society of Genealogists in London and his book was the first in general circulation. It has a certain stuffy charm but the changes in the genealogical world in the last fifteen years make it untrustworthy.

There are two general books I advise everyone to examine. The bestselling choice is George Pelling's *Beginning Your Family History*. Pelling is a television personality in England based on this book, which has sold more than 75,000 copies worldwide. He updates it every couple of years, too, so the material is fresh.

English genealogical expert Howard Rokeby-Thomas of Cambridge found Pelling's style not to his taste, but for beginners, the book is a good one. It explains the basics of English research well. For newcomers, that means civil registration, the census and parish records.

Civil registration began in England and Wales in 1837 and has always been more thoroughly handled than in Canada. You are more likely to find your ancestors' documents and to discover that they are very informative.

The census is much like Canada's, since both were designed by the same civil servants back in the 1840s. The complete 1891 census for England is held at the LDS family history center in Kitchener.

Church records at the parish level began 450 years ago and many parishes have registers going back to 1600. They are now, by law, in protected environments, mostly in county record offices and available only on microfilm. Many are also available through the LDS. You will not be able, as I was twenty years ago, to sit in a damp vestry on a stone seat looking at the originals taken from a centuries-old chest. It was fun, but it was also a good way to get bronchitis.

My own favorite among the general texts is *Tracing Your Family Tree*, by Jean A. Cole and Michael Armstrong. Cole is columnist for *Family Tree* magazine and her no-nonsense approach is for people who want more details than you will find in Pelling. In a country as old as England, there are many variations on the standard resources, especially as you push back to the eighteenth century. Cole seems to have everything at her fingertips, and is good for referrals to other books and addresses to send for more information.

My suggestion is that you will want to look over these possibilities at your local library before making a choice about which to buy for use at home. If you have much English research to do, you will want to have one of them at hand for quick reference. All four are still in print and available from genealogical booksellers as well as general bookstores.

(8 October 1994)

Calendars

A genealogist I know recently received a photocopied document from Alsace. It dated from the earliest years of the nineteenth century, when the effects of the French Revolution were still felt in France. One of these was the new system of dating. Her ancestor was born on the eighth day of the third decade of Brumaire, year ten.

Naturally, she wanted to convert this to our Gregorian calendar. Where could she turn?

The Book of Calendars is a reference tool which every researcher should know. You may not want to own one, but be familiar with its spot in your public library.

The Book of Calendars contains information and examples on calendars ancient and modern, including those used in Babylonia, Tyre, the Egypt of the Pharoahs and Tibet. These are interesting, but you may not need them.

At the back of the book is a large section which you will want time and again. There is an explanation of the French Revolutionary calendar. It does not include an easy chart for conversion, but enough information for you to do the calculation yourself.

In addition, there are perpetual Gregorian calendars, lists of when Easter falls, the church year and information on the Julian calendar. All of these have significance for genealogists.

If you want to determine what day of the week a family event occurred, you use a perpetual calendar. There are only a limited number of variations in the year. All are given, with a chart telling you which example corresponds to which year. Copies of the perpetual calendar used to be printed in the K-W telephone book, so you might have an old one around. If not, consult *The Book of Calendars*. (You may also find a calculator for these days on your genealogical software.)

Many old church records will refer to an event taking place on a particular day in the ecclesiastical year. Since church happenings were at the centre of everyone's life, the church year was the basis for organization. In England rents, taxes, employment and the payment of annuities all took place on the four quarter days: Lady Day (Feast of the Annunciation of Our Lady), Midsummer Day (St. John the Baptist), Michaelmas (St. Michael and All Angels) and Christmas. Lady Day was also, until 1752, the first day of the year. The year thus began in March, not January.

Quarter days in Scotland were different, including instead Candlemas (2 February), Whitsun (Pentecost) and Martinmas (St Martin of Tours, 11 November).

Most confusing of all, the old Julian calendar which had been in use for centuries had miscalculated the rounds of the sun and was out of synch with nature. In 1582, Pope Gregory skipped ten days (from October 5-14) to catch up. This was in effect in all Catholic countries immediately but the Protestant countries took some time to catch up. England made the change in 1752, when ten days in September were lost. Before that time, the year began in March and the days were different, so dates given in the Julian format are labelled "Old Style" or OS. Gregorian dates are "New Style" (NS).

If you think that those ten days are long forgotten, you are wrong. We all know that July 12 is remembered in Ireland for the Battle of the Boyne. When the first battle of the Somme (1 July 1916) resulted in the disappearance of the 9th Ulster Rifles through virtually all of the soldiers being killed or wounded, people pointed out that, under the Old Style, it was still July 12. The worst day in the Irish calendar had come back to haunt them.

A quick and easy dating reference is *Genealogical Dates: A User-Friendly Guide*, by Kenneth L. Smith. This is a new edition of his popular handbook, which includes all the genealogical calendars I have mentioned above. Even better, it comes with a computer disk to assist your computations. If it interests you, send US$19.50 to Olde Springfield Shoppe, Box 171, Elversen PA 19520-0171 USA.

The Book of Calendars is available in the reference department of the Kitchener library.

(25 October 1994)

The Father of All French-Canadians?

How would you react if someone said that all the Québécois in North America are descended from the same couple?

I was skeptical. These important ancestors are Zacharie Cloutier and his wife, Xainte Dupont. They emigrated from the Perche region of France in 1634, among the earliest settlers in Quebec. Appropriately for his name, Zacharie was a master carpenter. The Cloutiers came as workers on one of the new seigneuries but eventually held their own land at Chateau-Richer, not far from Quebec City. In fact, they lived in Lower Town Quebec for much of their lives.

They had six children, five of whom survived to accompany them to New France. There were three sons, Zacharie, Charles and Jean, and two daughters, Anne and Louise. Anne has a place in Canadian history as the bride in the first marriage contract made in the new land.

Anne was only ten when the contract was signed in 1636 with her father's boarder, Robert Drouin the brick-maker. The religious ceremony took

78

place when she was eleven, but she remained at home with her parents until the age of thirteen. She died at 22 in 1648, leaving two daughters. Robert Drouin is the ancestor of many others of that name by his second wife.

But were Zacharie and Xainte the ancestors of everyone? Thomas Laforest, the author of eighteen volumes of stories called *Our French-Canadian Ancestors*, says: "The genealogist Gabriel Drouin exaggerates only a little bit when he states that Zacharie Cloutier is the ancestor of all the French Canadians."

The explanation is that there were only a handful of settlers in those early days. They intermarried and their descendants ranged far and wide over the province. Eventually they settled throughout both Canada and the United States.

Zacharie's other daughter married a son of Abraham Martin, of Plains of Abraham fame. She left no children. However, the three sons produced many offspring, which accounts for all the Cloutiers we know. The descendants of one son, Jean, remained in the family homestead at Chateau-Richer for over three hundred years.

It seems likely that Zacharie and Xainte, along with the other couples who had healthy families in the early days of New France, can claim to be ancestors of all French-Canadians. Naturally, any serious genealogist will still want to verify their own descent from this interesting pair.

Thomas Laforest's series is a useful one. Each volume contains a series of biographical sketches of pioneers of Quebec. If you have ancestry there, you may want to check for your own family name. The stories are in English and each volume is indexed so names are easy to find. The series is available in many libraries or you can write directly to the publisher: Lisi Press, Box 1063, Palm Harbor FL 33563 USA.

Laforest ends his Cloutier story with a list of variant spellings of the name, some of which are surprising. One of them is Nailer, which looks completely different, but has the same meaning in English as Cloutier in French.

Anne Cloutier of Kitchener, who first told me about Zacharie, says that some members of the family spell their name Clouthier. This is usually a sign that they come from Northern Ontario or Manitoba. Her husband, Ray, has a theory that this spelling is the result of English-speakers who have added their own little bit to the name.

The Cloutiers have an annual reunion at Quebec City and there is a genealogist who tries to keep them all straight. They have a newsletter as well (published in French). If you would like to get in touch with them, write to l'Association des Cloutier d'Amérique, C.P. 2144, Quebec QC G1K 7N8. (22 November 1994)

Peel County & Avotaynu Magazine

When our ancestors sailed down the St. Lawrence River in search of cheap land, many of them did not know where to go. When they arrived in Toronto, many would stop on the way for a time to make money.

Peel County, which is west of Toronto, was a stopping place for numbers of families who eventually came to Wellington, Waterloo and Perth.

If your family had even temporary roots in Peel, you will be glad to know that Jan Speers' and Trudy Mann's useful set of indexes called *People of Peel* has been republished. Speers and Mann found a number of early documents which gave names of residents of Peel. They gathered the names and collected them in a series of indexes published in one book in 1981.

Materials indexed include some local histories, the 1843 Chinguacousy tax list and the 1877 atlas of the county. There are also church records included: Anglican records from Brampton 1851-1870, a Methodist mission 1843-1857, and strays from Peel married at St. James' cathedral in Toronto 1800-1896.

This last is a good reminder that many people wandered some distance from home to be married. People who lived near a big city were often tempted to go there for their wedding. The reason for this may have been as simple as the expense involved. After all, weddings were then (and still are) expensive. A trip to the clergyman's front parlor was not.

These indexes are worth checking. The original edition of *People of Peel* can be seen at the Kitchener public library. The new edition, published this April by Halton-Peel Branch, Ontario Genealogical Society, sells for $18.00. It is available from them at Box 70030, 2441 Lakeshore Road W., Oakville ON L6L 6M9.

Anyone with interests in Peel will want to use the 1877 atlas (also at KPL) and the huge county history. It is called simply *A History of Peel County* and was published in 1967 for Canada's centennial. There is also a short handbook for genealogical workers, *Research in Halton and Peel* (1983), by Jan Speers and Ruth Holt.

Some areas are lucky to have a historian with the combined instincts of a magpie and a packrat. Peel is one. William Perkins Bull gathered information about people and places in Peel throughout an interesting career in the area a century ago. His papers fill many archives boxes. They used to be at the Archives of Ontario but have now been transferred to the Peel regional archives in Brampton. It is unlikely anyone will want to use the originals, however, as they are all available on microfilm in both Brampton and Toronto.

The families in Perkins Bull are not confined to Peel, but are centred there. People with roots in Halton, Wentworth or the eastern part of Wellington would be advised to check the Perkins Bull papers for material on their ancestors. Some parts of the papers have been indexed but you will still want the fun of exploring the archives for yourself.

A hint for Eastern European researchers: The news about Eastern Europe never seems to end. I was talking Curt Witcher and he suggested that everyone with roots there should be aware of *Avotaynu, the review of Jewish genealogy.* Even if you are not Jewish, you will want to look at this interesting magazine, which always seems to be aware of what is happening now. The current issue includes information on Polish and Ukrainian archives, German laws regarding access to records, a new genealogical society in Lithuania, and advice about finding lost European relations in Bogota, Colombia and Mexico City.

Avotaynu should be available nearby, if it is not already. It costs $24 a year from Avotaynu Inc., 1485 Teaneck Road, Teaneck NJ 07666 USA. (29 November 1994)

Update: The Peel Archives published Wm. Perkins Bull: Guide to the Wm. Perkins Bull Records at the Region of Peel Archives *(1995), a very helpful starting place for working with this vast collection.*

✦

Good Advice for Starting Your Research

As we face a fresh year, let's take another look at starting your genealogy. Those who are experienced might still ask themselves if they follow this good advice.

Do not procrastinate. Get started now, simply by writing down what you know on a sheet of paper. You can organize it later. Too many people think they know "nothing". Most of us know a great deal.

Those who already have an idea how to work should proceed with it right away. I always remind myself of the time I wanted to see an old uncle's picture. I was in his daughter-in-law's house and she said, "Oh yes, it's upstairs. I'll get it down for you sometime." That was in 1966. I did not see the picture until 1987.

Organize. Once you have some basic information, put it on some genealogical forms. These are available from the Ontario Genealogical Society, the LDS family history center or a genealogical supply house. Seeing your information on the forms will show you where the holes are. It will point the way to your next research strategy.

Ask for help. We can all learn from others. Consult guides at your local public library and attend genealogical society meetings. There you will meet experts in various fields who are keen to offer you advice. If you are very lucky, you might even meet a cousin you did not know before.

If you get stuck once you have begun researching, do not hesitate to look to others for assistance. One of the most interesting aspects of family history is the network of researchers you will meet.

Don't assume anything. Perhaps the most common mistake that new genealogists make is to believe everything they hear from family legends. They also get a lot of exercise leaping to conclusions. They are heard to say, "It *must* be here."

Verify each fact as you go along, by looking at the original documents (not merely the indexes) and understanding everything they have to tell you. Do not be in too great a hurry. Concentrate, consider and be skeptical about anything that looks dubious.

Pass your findings around. Most of us are only too glad to talk about what we have discovered. Be sure to share what you know with other researchers, but also make a point of presenting copies of it to non-genealogical family members.

These handouts should be in a format they can understand. I do not recommend handing around family group sheets, which only genealogists can figure out. A family chart on one page, a three page story or brief biography, will be much appreciated, will stimulate discussion and may lead to your finding out even more than you hoped.

Do not give up. As you progress, the history will become more complex. You will also reach dead ends. These need not be permanent. What looks like the end now may merely reflect your inexperience or the fact that the information you seek lies in an obscure resource. Give it a rest and before you know it, some inspiration will set you on the right track again. This inspiration usually takes the form of reading genealogical journals or talking to experienced "genies" who can offer good counsel.

Whatever you do, **enjoy yourself.** This is a hobby with depths of pleasure that some people experience all their lives. You have a detective search, meeting people, travel, learning and the thrill of the chase.

Suggestions for the topics in this column came from *GeneAssist*, newsletter of the genealogical special interest group of American Mensa (May 1993 issue). If you are connected with Mensa and would like more interest on their genealogy group, write to Mark Hutchenreuter, 1831 Piedmont Street, Oxnard CA USA 93035-3523.

(3 January 1995)

Dufferin County

The Ontario Genealogical Society attempts to assign responsibility for every part of Ontario to one of its branches. Dufferin County is an exception.

Dufferin was formed in the 1880s from bits of Simcoe, Wellington and Halton counties. It is largely rural, with one sizable town, Orangeville.

Genealogists with interests in this area may find that they are unsure where to turn. The new Dufferin County Archives is the answer.

The Dufferin County Museum and Archives began in a small area in Orangeville a few years ago. In 1994, they moved into their own building on the northeast corner of highway 89 and Airport Road (County Road 18). The new facilities provide 2000 square feet of reading room as well as extensive exhibition halls.

The staff of the museum is active in collecting material on the county. They have both printed books and archival papers, including microfilm and family histories. Some things in the reading room, the microfilm guides, index printouts and family histories are self-serve. The staff are pleased to help you find the rare holdings.

A complete list of the cemeteries in Dufferin can be found in the OGS' guide to all the cemeteries in the province (available at the Kitchener library). Some of the cemeteries in East Garafraxa and East Luther have been transcribed by members of Waterloo-Wellington branch. Other cemeteries, including Forest Lawn in Orangeville have been transcribed privately. They are available at the Dufferin archives and the Kitchener library.

The archives staff have also produced some cemetery transcriptions themselves. Last year they published inscriptions for ten cemeteries in

Mulmur township in one volume. Information about all their publications can be obtained at the archives.

If you visit, be sure to see the museum as well. It includes a replica of a 1915 farmhouse, an Orange lodge display, Crombie's Station (a railway station of 1872) and cabinet work by county craftsmen. Large artifacts from the collection which are not in an exhibition can be viewed permanently in the a storage room on level one. This idea is a good one for all museums, ensuring that visitors see everything they can.

Although there is no cafe in the building, there is a restaurant across the street. The level four observation lounge in the museum offers stunning views over Mulmur and Mono. The drive there from K-W is through the marshy fields of north Wellington which are a pleasure in themselves.

Write to the Dufferin County Museum and Archives at RR #3, Mansfield ON L0N 1M0 or call for a brochure at 705-435-1881. The museum and archives are open 10-5 Tuesday to Saturday. The museum only is also open on Sunday afternoons.

Since Orangeville is the large center in the county, you should look at the newspaper there for obituaries or marriage announcements for your Dufferin families. Margaret Beettam, a member of Halton-Peel branch OGS has done considerable work indexing the *Orangeville Sun*.

Three volumes of index are currently available, covering 1860-1884, 1885-1894 and 1895-1899. You notice that the time periods get shorter as the years pass. This is because the population grows, the paper gets larger and more informative.

The index is a short and basic one, giving only the name, date and page of the item, with a code reference for the kind (birth, death, marriage, engagement or similar). It is a simple matter to track down your family from the Orangeville area. These indexes are available for sale at $23 each from Halton Peel Branch (Box 70030, Oakville ON L6L 1M9). You can also locate them for reference at the Dufferin archives or the Brampton public library (Chinguacousy branch).

Those interested in purchasing a copy of Forest Lawn Cemetery in Orangeville can do so from Alan Rayburn, 5 Solva Drive, Nepean ON K2H 5R4. The price is $18.

(31 January 1995)

The Irish At Home and Abroad

Have you ever seen a family tree that goes back to Adam and Eve? I have. They were commonly produced a century or more ago in that land of fable and fantasy, Ireland. Start with an ordinary Irishman, work back a few generations until things get misty. Produce an earl or even a duke to make things interesting. By the time you get back a thousand years, everyone is descended from Brian Boru, one of the greatest of Irish heroes. Keep on going and eventually you get to Adam and Eve.

I never knew why the Irish had a special handle on these genealogies, more than, say, the Swiss or the Swedes. An article in the first edition of *The Irish At Home and Abroad* explained why.

The Irish At Home and Abroad is an interesting new genealogical magazine produced in Salt Lake City. It is not connected with the Mormon church or the Family History Library. Its stated purpose is, "to provide informative and realistic articles for the genealogist."

Having examined a few issues, I can say that it succeeds. There are library profiles, information about resources in various Irish counties, book reviews and facts about the Irish abroad. Issue #2 has an article entitled "The Irish in Montreal."

The basic facts, sometimes neglected in other periodicals, are always there. Addresses, telephone numbers and lists of book titles seem to be on every page. This is especially useful for the Irish addresses, which may be difficult to find in Canada.

Issue #3 says that there is a controversy over who can say they are "Black Irish." Did your family use this term? The editors ask for readers' input on what they meant.

A sprightly article on Irish names tells of a search for Delia Holland in County Cork records. Only by the use of some generous expertise was it finally established that she had started life as Bridget Houlihan. Bridget, it seems, has fifteen variations, including Breda, Bessie, Dina and Phidelia. Only the Irish would know.

At one time, the Irish forms of family names were not allowed, which meant that there was an English form. In old records, the original might be used. That is how Houlihan became Holland.

The test of a genealogical magazine is that it provides something for everyone in each issue. *The Irish At Home and Abroad* manages very well. The emphasis always on giving the reader something to think about.

What about Adam and Eve? The Irish believed that kingship descended straight from God via Adam. There were several kingdoms in Ireland, and all those kings had to establish their divine right to hold the throne. The fanciful genealogies were the result, taken more seriously there than elsewhere.

Magazines from many of the Irish family history societies are rather local in nature. If you have always wanted to subscribe to something which will broaden your knowledge of the Irish genealogical scene, this magazine may be the one you need. Its appeal is such that I would recommend it to societies or libraries who want to add an inexpensive subscription to their list. It will also be indexed in PERSI, the genealogical magazine index which will add to its appeal. PERSI is available at the Kitchener library.

The Irish at Home and Abroad is published at Box 521806, Salt Lake City UT USA 84152. Subscriptions to Canada cost US$16.00.

To end on an Irish note, here is an old Irish prayer which came my way today: "Let those that love us, love us. And those that don't love us, may God turn their hearts. And if he doesn't turn their hearts, may he turn their ankles, so we may know them by their limping."
(7 February 1995)

The Family Historian's Enquire Within

If you are researching family members in a faraway place, I always recommend you begin by buying a genealogical handbook for the area.

Sometimes you need more than that. Especially when doing British research, I find that there are phrases or ideas which I need to interpret quickly and which the handbooks do not discuss in detail. If you are interested in English research, there is a book to help you.

The Family Historian's Enquire Within, by Pauline Saul and F. C. Markwell comes in the form of a dictionary. Each entry is brief, but gives a succinct definition and account of the topic concerned. If you are interested in a particular kind of record, it will describe how to find it.

For example, my Devonshire ancestors lived on the estates of Lord Rolle, the largest landowner in the county. The Rolles are extinct now, but I wondered what happened to their family papers. A quick check under "manorial records" in the *Enquire Within* told me that a country-wide index of manuscripts and archives is kept by the National Register of Archives in London. In addition, the authors recommended two resource books which would prepare me for using manorial records and two more for background

86

reading. In every case, they gave the address necessary to find either the National Register or the books.

This works well. The Rolle papers are at the Devon County Record Office in Exeter, which is top of my list of places to visit when I am next in England.

Topics from the most basic to the more obscure are given space by Saul and Markwell. You can begin dealing with the complex topic of wills or learn the meaning of your ancestor's trade. My favourite is "maker-up", which has nothing to do with cosmetics. In the textile industry, it is a person who sews garments together, but can also be a druggist.

This book has gone through several editions. In its early stages it was a slim volume entitled *The Family Historian's A-Z*. The new title, based on a familiar book of household cures from Victorian times, is now famous on both sides of the Atlantic. Pauline Saul is the administrator of the Federation of Family History Societies and at the centre of genealogical life in Britain. The current edition of the *Enquire Within* appeared in 1994.

As well as explaining all those strange phrases, the *Enquire Within* provides maps of the counties of England and Wales (before and after 1974), Scotland (before and after 1975), and the Republic of Ireland (after 1922).

There are brief listings for the archival holdings of the Public Record Offices at both Kew and Chancery Lane and a chronology of British regiments, for those about to embark on the murky waters of military record searching.

This book is one which needs to be by the elbow of every British genealogist. I use mine often. It is available from SEL Enterprises, Box 92, Thornhill ON L3T 3N1. You can also consult it in the reference department of the Kitchener library.

The changes in county borders in Britain in 1974-5 caused unfamiliar genealogists a great deal of grief. A few weeks ago, the local government authority in London announced that it was changing the borders again.

Many of those who 'lost' their counties in 1974 have never given up hope that they would get them back. Now some of them are. Both Rutland and Herefordshire are being restored. There is also talk of bringing back the three ridings of Yorkshire. If your family came from one of the counties which vanished twenty years ago, watch for changes which will affect where you have to write for information, or where you need to go to do research.
(28 February 1995)

1869-1873 Marriages in Ontario

When the Ontario civil registration records became available three years ago, one of the great advantages were the computer generated indexes which make it possible to locate the record you want in minutes.

Unfortunately, the earliest records were not as well organized as succeeding years. The first four years of records (1869-1873) had old hand-written indexes which were hard to read and often left the impression that they were incomplete.

Genealogists who use the Archives of Ontario records regularly have often expressed the hope that someone would reindex these records, thus guaranteeing that the most important civil registration records would be as accessible as possible.

Renie Rumpel of Kitchener decided to undertake the task. Her company, Ontario Indexing Services, has recently published the first volume in the series, *Index to Marriage Registrations of Ontario Canada, 1869-1873*. It covers the first four volumes of the registrations.

She tells me that once the indexing had begun, she noticed that there were many problems with the old handwritten indexes. Names were missing or misspelled. Dates had been omitted. In the microfilming of the records, pages had been missed, which meant those registrations were virtually lost. Worst of all, whole volumes of the registrations had been missed from the index.

Ontario Indexing Services sets this right by starting at the beginning again.

Names are indexed according to the way they appear in the registrations themselves. This is the only solution. We have mentioned before in this column that family names were often spelled in different ways throughout the nineteenth century. Standardized spelling of names has only begin with our own century.

"It's interesting to see that often a name is indexed two or three ways in different volumes. The Registrar must have had difficulty reading the names as he used different spellings for the parents and witnesses in the same record," says Rumpel.

To keep the index books a reasonable size, they have chosen to index only the names of bride and groom, the date and location.

Rumpel says this fits with the other computerized indexes for later years of the vital records. An index which included all the information would be four to five times larger and would have a correspondingly higher price.

In the end, there are 75,000 names waiting to be indexed. The first volume, which is now in print, contains 12,100 entries.

Once you have the index record, it is possible to access the original registration using the Archives of Ontario microfilm. This is available every day at the AO in Toronto. It can also be used through the LDS family history center at Lorraine and River road in Kitchener or through the interlibrary loan facilities of your public library. There are also LDS family history centers in Guelph and Owen Sound.

Aside from the value of this index, one of the most intriguing additions to the first volume is a gazetteer of the locations where the marriages occurred. Rumpel has provided an alphabetical listing of the towns and townships, with maps to show where they are. Also included is a map showing rail and steamship lines of the time.

The addition of these geographical details will be a great help to anyone using the index, especially those who are not as familiar with places in Ontario.

This book is an exciting addition to the materials available for early Canadian research. I will be keeping my copy within easy reach.

Volume 1 of the Index to *Marriage Registrations of Ontario Canada 1869-1873* is available for $25 including postage and packing. Write to Ontario Indexing Services at 351 Pommel Gate Crescent, Waterloo N2L 5X7. (4 April 1995)

Update: Renie Rumpel's set of six volumes covering 1869-1873 was completed in 1996. The price of each volume is $25, from the address above. Meanwhile, other extracters and indexes have turned their attention to these marriages. A sample is given below:

Grey County Marriages, 1869-1873

Interest in the 1869-1873 marriage registrations continues. Although Renie Rumpel's *Index to Marriage Registrations of Ontario, Canada 1869-1873* is now complete in six volumes, individual sections of these hard to read records are being published elsewhere for smaller areas.

Grey County Marriages: Marriage Registrations for Grey County, Ontario from 1869 to 1873, by Jeff Stewart and Sherilyn Bell was recently published by Winfield Press in Toronto. It includes complete abstracts of the official documents for more than a thousand marriages. Details on how to consult the original handwritten records is also included.

Cost is $30.50 postpaid, from Winfield Press, 1000 Gerrard Street East, Box 98206, Toronto M4M 3L9.
(20 May 1997)

A Guide to Illness and Disease

Even if you already know when an ancestor died, make a point of obtaining the relevant death certificate. You never know what it will tell you.

After the release of the early Ontario civil registration records three years ago, I brought out my old family histories and began to look up everyone's death certificate. I hit the jackpot with a 1916 record of a great-great-aunt, which gave her exact birthplace. It linked my family with another of the same name, which opened a new avenue of research.

The most common new fact you will discover is the cause of death of your relations. In this day of growing fascination with genetically-transmitted illnesses, the material you uncover may be vitally important.

Many of the causes of death will be merely "old age" or its synonym, "decay of nature", which may be uninformative. Others will be more useful.

Interpreting them is another matter. The names of diseases have varied over the years, and some illnesses do not even exist any more. Have you heard of anyone dying of "brain fever" lately?

What do you do when you encounter "phthisis"? Was someone who had "jolly rant" enjoying himself? My godmother keeps hoping to find a relation who had "quinsy," which sounds more like a doll's name.

A recent Canadian book will help you understand what you find on death certificates and also provides a brief history of the practice of medicine over the past centuries. The next time you feel unhappy with your doctor, consider the past and you will thank him for being so kind.

A Family Historian's Guide to Illness, Disease and Death Certificates, by Elizabeth Briggs devotes a quarter of the text to the way medicine was practised, beginning in ancient times. In the past, dentists and pharmacists had greater influence in medical matters. Many patent medicines were considered useful for a broad spectrum of illnesses, and people would consult the druggist for help rather than go to the doctor. People often had faith that these cure-alls would do the trick for whatever ailed them.

In her list of diseases, Briggs cross-references the many variant names to the most common one. It is here that we learn that "phthisis" is another name for tuberculosis. A person suffering from "jolly rant" had influenza.

Toward the end of the book, Briggs gives examples of death certificates from a variety of places. She reminds us that when we receive a new death certificate we should look at every piece of information on it for any genealogical clues which it might hold. This is true of any document we research. Even the ink smudges or the blank spaces might tell us something.

She supplies us with a full listing of addresses where death certificates can be obtained in Canada and Britain. In the United States, most states have a central civil registration office, but the quickest place to obtain a death certificate is the county courthouse.

This book is a useful reference work but it also contains enough miscellaneous information on health subjects that you could spend a happy afternoon merely browsing in its pages. I was glad to have it when I was sent the death certificate of a young great-aunt with an almost illegible cause of death. Elizabeth Briggs told me that she had died, aged 3, of tuberculosis.

A Family Historian's Guide to Illness, Disease and Death Certificates, by Elizabeth Briggs, can be ordered for $19.75 from Westgarth, 46 Burnhill Bay, Winnipeg MB R3T 5N3.

As for quinsy, it is an almost forgotten name for that universal childhood ailment, tonsillitis. More than a century ago, it was sometimes fatal.
(11 April 1995)

Tunkers or Brethren in Christ

The small denomination of churches known as Brethren in Christ has a long history in our area.

The original Brethren in Christ began in Maryland and Pennsylvania and mainly grew out of evangelical German pioneer meetings there. However, early settlers in our area were known as Tunkards (or Tunkers, or Dunkers). Their religion began in Germany. It had a connection with the neighbouring Amish and Mennonites, and also with the Baptists in terms of its theology and some of its practices.

Their small congregations were self-governing but as time passed they wished to join together. Eventually they became part of the Brethren in Christ.

There were many more Brethren churches in Waterloo County in the nineteenth century than there are now. There was even an academy associated with the denomination at Bridgeport, and the clergy who taught there ventured into the countryside on weekends holding services in many villages in the northern part of the county.

In 1907, the United Brethren in Christ in Canada merged with the Congregational Churches (now part of the United Church of Canada). Some of the UBC churches (such as that in Roseville) remained independent.

Many of the Dunker churches had become Mennonite in one form or another, and as they developed they called themselves Brethren in Christ. This quick overview does not do justice to the complex history of these churches, but it should be emphasized that the United Brethren in Christ and the present-day Brethren in Christ churches did not grow from the same origins.

As with other self-governing evangelical congregations, many of these churches kept few records. Little survives for the genealogist to use, but some scraps remain. There are no known records from the academy in Bridgeport, except the reports which clergy there submitted on marriages performed in the years 1858-1869. These cover a broad region in the county. The original submissions are available on microfilm at the Kitchener library, and are indexed.

If you have an interest in the history of the Brethren, E. Morris Sider's *The Brethren in Christ in Canada: Two Hundred Years of Tradition and Change* (1988) will provide the background you want.

If your ancestors were Tunkers, you may want to find out more about them. Mary Shupe Shantz's article "Discovering the Tunkers" appeared in the 1984 edition of the Waterloo Historical Society's annual volume. The magazine *Ontario History* published "The Early Years of the Tunkers in Upper Canada," by E. Morris Sider in its volume 51 (1959). Shantz' description of the Tunkers' love-feasts, one of their principal religious rites, is especially intriguing for modern researchers.

All of the above are available at the Kitchener library.

The American Tunkers are now called The Church of the Brethren (who are quite distinct from the remaining Brethren in Christ). They have an historical organization which may be of assistance to those whose ancestors were Tunkers, because many of our Tunker families originated in Pennsylvania.

Their historical committee publishes two free pamphlets which researchers may want to see. One is called "Guide to Research in Brethren History" and the other "Guide to Research in Brethren Family History." The first is largely a bibliography of available materials. The second offers advice on how to do family history with an emphasis on Brethren documents, and particularly addresses the fact that many church records have not survived.

You can contact the Fellowship of Brethren Genealogists at 1451 Dundee Avenue, Elgin IL USA 60120 to obtain copies of these pamphlets. Please send a long stamped, self-addressed envelope. The stamp should be from the US post office, or use an international reply coupon.

Another branch of the Brethren has a good deal of its historical material at Messiah College in Grantham, Pennsylvania. The collection there was developed by Morris Sider, who is the authority on Canadian Brethren history.

(9 May 1995)

The Scottish Collection at the University of Guelph

Are you hoping to do some Scottish research? The prospect of visiting Edinburgh is enticing, but costly. You can begin by driving to the University of Guelph.

The Scottish collection in Guelph was begun in 1965. Its purpose is to support graduate programs in various disciplines. The collection was begun by the History Department and is rich in historical materials.

If you visit the University of Guelph library, you will not find the Scottish collection in one location. It numbers 100,000 volumes and is scattered through the building. The result is a world-wide reputation for Scottish studies, primarily for academics but of benefit to family historians as well.

At the recent Ontario Genealogical Society weekend seminar in Chatham, Carol Goodger-Hill of Kitchener outlined some of the resources which might interest genealogists. She is a librarian in the government documents section of the library.

She recommends that you begin by looking at an introductory text on Scottish genealogy, such as Kathleen Cory's *Tracing Your Scottish Ancestry*. I also like Alwyn James' *Scottish Roots*.

UG has gazetteers and maps which will help you locate your ancestral village. Make sure you know the area by studying a map before you go to the records, otherwise you may make mistakes.

Although UG does not have the Scottish census, it is available locally through the LDS family history center.

One interesting geographical aid is Sir John Sinclair's *Statistical Account of Scotland*. It describes the various parishes giving details of local worthies, the land and buildings, from information supplied by the local Presbyterian clergy. The data supplied varies according to the man giving it, but if your ancestors lived in a particular place, you will have a full description of their surroundings.

Enlarging on this theme, there are local histories from many places. Carol points out that many of these contain lists of local people or those who held offices in the parish government. They are also illustrated with the kind of pictures you might find useful.

The history of Callandar, originally published in the early nineteenth century, set out to be interesting above all. Catherine Ferguson was included because of her enormous size and Charlie Duff because he was a talented storyteller. A surprising mention of someone in your family may be in their local history.

The library also has a variety of Scottish directories, many from the nineteenth century when our ancestors were living there before their emigration. Some of these are professional listings, others street directories similar to those we still see here.

Scottish family history societies have not been as active as their English or Canadian confreres in transcribing gravestones, but UG has the published volumes that are available.

If you are unsure of where your ancestor originated, try consulting Donald Whyte's *Dictionary of Scottish Emigrants to Canada Before Confederation*. Whyte includes places of origin and names of parents. This book is also available at the Kitchener library, and a second volume is being prepared for publication in 1996.

In terms of difficulty, Scottish genealogy lies somewhere between the wealth of material available in England and the empty cabinets we find in Ireland. The tiny population in a wild countryside probably accounts for this.

However, genealogists in western Ontario are fortunate in having an exciting collection such as that at the University of Guelph library which they can use if they cannot go to Scotland itself. In fact, those planning a trip to Edinburgh should probably do what they can in Guelph, leaving only the more difficult searches for those precious hours over the sea.

If you wish to ask if the university has a particular title, call them at 1-824-4120.

(27 June 1995)

Update: The second volume of Donald Whyte's Dictionary of Scottish Emigrants to Canada *was published on schedule in 1996. As well, the Aberdeen area Family History Society has recently published many cemeteries.*

94

The Marsh Collection, Amherstburg

Local history was once the specialty of amateur historians. Genealogists everywhere can be grateful to people who were interested enough to begin collecting material that might otherwise have vanished.

A common place to look for bits of history has always been the local newspaper. Especially in small towns, there seems to have been someone who wrote and gathered the facts we cherish.

In Amherstburg, near Windsor, the local newspaper was the *Echo*. It was owned by the Marsh family for 85 years. For sixty of those years, John Marsh and his sister Helen wrote columns of local information as well as owning and managing the paper.

In the course of their researches, they collected a great many archival documents, which included books and photographs.

As with all collectors, the Marshes had to face what would happen to their archives when they no longer had need of it. Realizing its value to their community, they decided to leave it in a form which would benefit everyone. The result is a foundation which runs the archives and makes it available to the public.

The Marsh Collection Society is located at 235A Dalhousie Street, Amherstburg ON N9V 1W6. The reading room is open on Mondays, Wednesdays and Fridays from 9 to 4:30. There is no charge for use of the research materials.

If you have interests in the area of the lower Detroit River (on the Canadian side, of course), you should investigate this collection.

As well as the original Marsh collections, the current curators have added to the materials available, which are now being accessed on a computer-based catalogue.

The original bound copies of the *Amherstburg Echo* for 1950 to 1990 are available. Older copies (1875-1949) are nearby in the Park House Museum at 214 Dalhousie Street. Other early newspapers published in Sandwich (Windsor) 1831-1852 are available on microfilm at the Marsh collection.

They also have the census microfilms for Essex county 1851-1901, the Essex county atlas (1881) and the *Commemorative Biographical Record for Essex County* (1905).

This last book is a very large digest of biographical sketches of local people. It was one of a series published in the United States at the turn of the century. Most of the volumes concerned American counties, but the publishers did venture over the border to produce books on Essex, Kent and Lambton counties. If your family lived in any of these, you should have a look. A researcher I know recently used one to discover a whole family of cousins. Included was a description of exactly where they had lived as they emigrated across the country.

The Marsh collection has files on local families and a great deal of information on the marine history of the Great Lakes, particularly in the Detroit River area. I am often asked questions about those elusive ancestors who sailed the lakes. This might be one place to look.

The Marsh collection found its home and finally opened its doors only in the autumn of 1994. It is a small collection with a clear focus, but no doubt its reputation will grow.

The first step in that growth has already occurred. *With The Tide: Recollections and Anecdotal Histories of the Town of Amherstburg and the Lower Detroit River District*, by John A. Marsh is its first publication. It is a collection of columns from the Amherstburg Echo written by the founder of the archives. It is available from the Marsh Collection Society for $25.

If you decide to visit, telephone ahead for an appointment, keeping in mind that this is, for the moment, a small place. The number is 1-736-9191. (4 July 1995)

The Maritime History Archive

If you wanted information about sailors, it might make sense to look for them in Newfoundland. What might surprise you is that you can look in St. John's for information about many British and American sailors as well.

Some time ago, the Public Record Office in London, England, found they were running out of room for certain kinds of records. Among these were information about shipping, including crewlists. They sought another institution which would take on the task of caring for these records and they were accepted by Memorial University of Newfoundland.

The Maritime History Archive there has accumulated a great deal more than these British documents. There are archival resources on the history of Newfoundland which will be of interest to those whose families originated there. It is interesting that Waterloo region perhaps has a larger concentration of Newfoundlanders than any other area of Ontario. This began with the workers who came to run the textile mills during World War II and stayed on, followed by members of their families.

Keith Matthews, a professor at MUN who was instrumental in founding the collection, spent much of his time collecting data on individuals who worked in the fisheries of Newfoundland. His files are now available for researchers.

This means that there are two kinds of genealogical work that we can do at MUN. One has to do with the fisher folk of the island, which means most families.

The other are the ships' lists. Since so many people are searching for passenger lists, I should emphasize that these are not at MUN. The lists in St. John's concern sailors, who are often difficult to trace because their lives took them all over the world.

If your ancestor was a British commercial sailor (as opposed to being in the navy), you should read Michael and Christopher Watts' *My Ancestor was a Merchant Seaman*, published by the Society of Genealogists.

There is the proverbial joke about the sailor who had a wife in every port. Multiple marriages of this kind may have happened more than we know. Tracing a sailor when you do not know his place of origin or which of many ports he will land at next can be impossible. My own sailor ancestor drowned in a very dramatic accident, thus leaving me an extra informative death certificate.

A Guide to the Holdings of the Maritime History Archive, by Roberta Thomas and Heather Wareham (1993) is a brief listing of the many files available. It does not contain as much detail as we might like, but we are told there are many finding aids created to assist those using individual files. There is also a card file in the reading room at the Maritime History Archive which contains many names.

Having noted that there are materials about eastern Canada and Britain, I can also say there are many files on other places, including New England. For example, the Benjamin Knight file contains the names of hundreds of fishermen, maritime artisans and labourers, mostly from Marblehead, Mass.

There are also unexpected genealogical materials. For instance, there are 41 reels of microfilm containing Irish parish records. Clare, Cork, Derry, Kerry, Kilkenny, Waterford and Wexford are included.

Because the port where the ships originated was also of interest, the collection includes many British newspapers on microfilm. The possibility of seeing these in Canada instead of England is an advantage. A quick look in the catalog shows entries for the Bristol Mirror and Liverpool Telegraph.

You might combine a visit to the Maritime History Archive with a tour of Newfoundland, which offers many activities for your non-genealogical family members. Write ahead to make an appointment or for more information: Maritime History Archive, Memorial University of Newfoundland, St. John's NF A1B 3Y1.

(11 July 1995)

More: Hints about the extent of Keith Matthews' family files can be found in his A "Who was Who" of Families Engaged in the Fishing and Settlement of Newfoundland, 1660-1840 *(1971). It includes names and locations of the families, and places where they originated in Britain, if known.*

The Loiselle Index: Marriages in Quebec

If you are looking for a marriage in Quebec, but are not sure where it took place, you may still be in luck.

Although civil registration in Quebec did not start until 1926, all marriages in Quebec had to be in church until 1969. This means that the parish registers are, in effect, civil registers too.

Genealogists have good reason to be grateful to Antonin Loiselle, a priest who spent his leisure time transcribing and indexing marriage records. As he worked in various parts of the province, he was able to access records from many parishes. He kept a card index of many thousands of names. In all, 460 parishes' registers are included.

The original index was stored at a Dominican convent in Montreal, but has been microfilmed by the Genealogical Society of Utah. It is now available through the LDS family history centers, at the National Archives in Ottawa, the Archives nationales du Québec in Quebec city (and its regional centers) and the Montreal Public Library. It occupies more than 150 reels of film.

Because of their civil nature, these church records were scrupulously kept. As Roland Auger says, "As the marriage acts always give the name of the parents of the husband and wife, the French Canadian genealogists trace the family back by the marriages, and, when they have time to do so, they then complete the story by the baptisms and burials." For this reason, the marriage volumes of the church records are frequently published first.

If you consult Loiselle, you can expect to find the names of the bride and groom, all four of their parents and the place of the wedding. You should also look at the original, for even Loiselle made mistakes. There, you will also find the names of the witnesses.

No matter where you research, you should always examine the names of the witnesses to weddings. Then, as now, these were frequently family members and can be clues to relationships you will establish later.

If you know the parish where your ancestors lived, you may simply want to look at the church records. Twenty years ago, you would have had to use microfilm of the original records, but the research can be done much more quickly now using the transcribed versions. These are usually published by local genealogical societies.

These church books are known as Repertoires and many hundreds of volumes are available. They will be listed under the name of the village, which is usually also the name of the church.

Another document exists for most marriages in Quebec before 1970. These are the notarial records.

Before marrying, couples would visit the local notary to sign a marriage contract. Their immediate family members would also be there. These documents, which were civil contracts concerning the property each brought to the marriage, are on file in the regional archives. Many of them have also been published. The earliest transcription was for Beauce. Brother Eloi-Gérard, another prominent collector of genealogical information, issued those for Charlevoix.

Recently, many more of these have become available either on microfilm in their original form or in indexes. If you use the indexes, remember to go back to look at the originals.

In many ways, researchers in Quebec have an easier time of it than their fellows in English Canada, because the church records, which are vital, are also so well kept. In a future column, we will look at other aspects of genealogy in Quebec.

Genealogists wishing to make telephone queries at the Archives nationales du Québec or the Montreal Public Library should remember they will need to conduct their calls in French. Angus Baxter says the Montreal central library is "fast becoming the main center for genealogical research in the province."

(8 August 1995)

Finding a Birth Mother

Frances Hoffman of West Montrose writes asking for assistance in finding a friend's birth mother. This adoption was forced by circumstance, and took place when the child was a little older, so the child has some information about her family.

Elena Benyes was born in Winnipeg in 1959. Her mother was 17 or so at the time of her birth, and Hungarian. She had come with her family to Canada, possibly from a displaced persons' camp (as they were known then) in Europe. Her family consisted of a mother, brother and sister. The father had died during the war. Elena's grandmother later remarried.

You have a scrap or two of good information, the most important of which is the family name.

Begin by searching in directories. City directories are a good first place to look. The Winnipeg directory for the late 1950s and 1960s was published by Henderson Directories in Vancouver. Copy out all the Benyes entries. Although the city is large, and Benyes is a relatively common Hungarian name, the families may be related. In particular, try to find a family which fits your description: a mother and three children in the same household.

Compare the Benyes entries from an old directory with the current one (available at the Kitchener library). Are any of the Benyes entries the same? It might be worthwhile giving them a call.

Telephone directories are also useful. Old directories are available on microfiche. Ten years ago, the Bell company archives in Montreal microfilmed all its directories and distributed copies of the fiche around the country, to make it easier for these kind of searches to take place. You may have to look farther afield to find the Manitoba directories, since Manitoba Telephone is a separate company.

However, keep in mind that there are only two telephone books for all of Manitoba. One is for Winnipeg and the other is for all the rest. This will make it simpler to search, if your family members moved out of the city.

Frances asks if citizenship and immigration records are available. The answer is probably not. Our government regards many of these records as private, and many of them have been destroyed. Unless you have more information to start with, this is not a fruitful path to follow.

The fact that this family was Hungarian is especially useful. Whenever you are pursuing a family of a particular ethnic group, use that as a lever to locate relations.

The National Archives has published a series of books listing resources of various ethnic groups held in Ottawa. The materials available are varied and from all over the country. The title of each volume in the series begins *Archival Resources for the study of....* Check to see if the Hungarian volume is available in a library nearby.

Many ethnic groups have both a club and a newspaper. If there is a Hungarian club in Winnipeg, they may also have a newspaper. I would get in touch with them, tell them the situation and ask if they would put a news item in the newsletter describing your situation. A family member may notice it, or someone who was a friend or neighbour thirty-five years ago may remember. They may ask you to place a paid advertisement instead (as the newspaper probably will).

The name and address of any ethnic newspaper in Canada can be found in directories of newspapers available in the reference section of your public library. There are general directories for newspapers all over North America, and particular listings of ethnic publications. Keep in mind that the ethnic newspaper read in one city may be published in another. Ask the Hungarian club where their Hungarian newspaper comes from.

High school yearbooks have been suggested as a possibility, and they may work, but that will require a trip to Winnipeg. If you decide to go there to look at them, ensure the library has collected them before you go. Many libraries were not saving high school yearbooks at that time.

If you find that a certain church was the centre for Hungarians in Winnipeg, you might try looking at their marriage records for any of the four weddings in the family. The birth mother herself, her mother, brother or sister may appear there.

Of all these, the best suggestion is the Hungarian club or clubs. Archival resources are useful for finding lost people, but the human memory is the quickest place to find clues.

(29 August 1995)

National Library on the Net

I dropped in for a visit at the National Library in Ottawa recently. The librarians there had some news.

The National Library now offers services on the Internet. Researchers who have access to this exciting new tool might find it useful to have a look at the National Library's home page.

If you do link up with them, you will find descriptions of their new publications, collections and services, cultural events and exhibitions. Best of all, they point you toward other Canadian internet information resources. The National Library will create links between the World Wide Web service and its continuing service on the Gopher.

For those of you who are new to the Internet (as I am myself), institutions begin by having a "home page". This serves as an introduction, often offering a menu of other possibilities. Key phrases and ideas are highlighted, and by choosing one of them, you can go deeper into the information available. You will find that at each step, there are more choices, and you can proceed, step by step, into the material.

This is very exciting, if a little bewildering at first. There is so much information on the Internet, the beginning reader hardly knows where to look. In addition, it is in a format many of us are not used to. Do not give up. Once you practise a little, you will find it comes more easily.

The National Library hopes to offer a wide variety of information about itself, and they think of the Internet as a better way to reach external clients. These are the many National Library users who are spread across the country and do not come to the reading room in person. In addition, they hope that people who are planning visits to Ottawa will look at their home page and the information they will provide there so that they are better prepared once they arrive.

They will be including copies of their pathfinders and lists of reference tools. Pathfinders are brief discussions of particular subject areas, giving titles of books which will be useful, and providing search strategies for finding more.

They will also be providing news about products and services, and a quick fact sheet which answers the "most asked questions". It might save you telephoning or writing the library itself.

One advantage that the Internet has over printed versions of the same information is that it can be easily updated on a regular basis. The information you find there may well be the most recent available.

Some of the material you find will be surprising. For example, using the National Library's home page and its links to other institutions, you will discover that the University of Toledo has an extensive Canadian genealogy section. No one would have thought this likely.

Paula Tallim explained to me that the philosophy of the Internet is to "get it up there and see who comments." As a result, the information is fresh and often unusual. You have to judge for yourself if everything you see is trustworthy. This makes surfing the Internet even more fun.

And there is fun on the home page of the National Library, too. Computer people always seem to have a sense of humor. Have a look at the graphics and facts. They change the jokes, as well as the news, regularly.

Researchers will want to know if the National Archives is also launched on the Internet, and the answer is: Not yet. However, the National Library gopher provides a network to other library catalogues which will enable us to search for the books we need without leaving home. We will have more to tell you about this side of the Internet in the future.

The Kitchener public library does not yet have an Internet terminal available to the public, but one is in the planning stage. The University of Waterloo library hopes to have limited Internet access for the public within the next few weeks. The National Library will be included.

(5 September 1995)

Update: The National Library's website address is http://www.nlc-bnc.ca. Perhaps the greatest advantage of the website is easy access to the National Library's catalogue from home. After initial difficulties in accessing the NL catalogue, I now find it easy, and can determine what they have in a moment.

The Kitchener library now has an Internet terminal for the public, as do most other larger libraries.

Upper Canada District Marriage Registers

The past few years has seen great advances in the accessibility of old Ontario marriage records.

The records have always been there. They are in manuscript form at the Archives of Ontario in Toronto. Finding the marriage you want may be difficult if you are unsure where or when it took place.

A decade ago, the 1858-1869 county marriages were published by Generation Press. Now, their predecessors, the district marriage registers, are being indexed and published for easy access.

Dan Walker of Delhi is working with a colleague, Robert Calder, to index the district marriage books. Some of the books have been indexed or published in full before, notably the ones for the easternmost counties. They were published in the *Ontario Register* bit by bit fifteen years ago. For those who are interested, the *Ontario Register* is available in its entirety at the Kitchener library.

Now, Walker is making the task simpler by reproducing the entries from the registers and indexing them. He includes the name of the clergyman and witnesses.

Experienced researchers realize that these names may be useful clues in tracing the exact location of our ancestors' homes. The witnesses are often family members.

If we know the clergyman's name, we can discover what church our ancestors were connected with, and then search their records for other family events.

Until the early 1830s, the government restricted who could perform marriages in Upper Canada (as Ontario was then called). Following the English example, only Anglican clergy were allowed to marry people.

In Canada, exceptions were made if there were no Anglican clergy nearby, and special licenses were granted to other clergy who lived in remote areas.

The law changed with the reform bill of 1832 in England. However, the government felt it wanted some control, to ensure that marriages were properly documented. After all, they were not merely religious or personal ceremonies, they were also civil contracts which affected inheritance and the sale of land.

Clergy of many denominations were licensed to perform marriages, but they were required to send reports of their activities to the government. The weddings they sent in were copied into ledgers which acted as official registrations.

The state of the provincial bureaucracy was such that many of these registrations were done in a haphazard way, so the district marriage books are not the easiest records to use.

In addition, some materials simply went astray. I remember in the early 1970s reading in the Toronto newspapers that a record book had been found behind a desk in the government bindery. It was being held there for a time, but was available to the public.

I went to see it, and found the second marriage of a great-great-grandfather in 1848. It is the only document which states the maiden name of his second wife. I have often wondered what became of that little minister's book.

Dan Walker's transcriptions will ease the burden of many genealogists who are searching for marriages in pre-1850 Ontario. Most of the volumes begin in the mid-1830s and go through to 1857.

He has begun publishing the volumes for western Ontario. The districts of Talbot, Brock, Huron, London and Bathurst are now available, at $21.95 a volume. London district requires two volumes. Newcastle district is announced for fall publication.

Since these books are organized by district rather than county, you will need to know which of the old districts your ancestors lived in. If you need help, enquire at your local library.

Write to Walker at NorSim Research and Publishing, 157 Ann St., Delhi N4B 1H8. Ask for a publications list, as NorSim also makes available many transcribed church records from Norfolk and Oxford counties.

(19 September 1995)

Update: Newcastle and Johnstown districts are now available.

Genealogical Writing

This is the perfect time of year to think about a writing project to keep you going through the winter months.

At the Federation of Genealogical Societies conference in Seattle, I attended a lecture entitled "Still Unpublished After All These Years." It describes the state of so many genealogists.

The lecturer was Jim Warren of Minneapolis, one of the leading genealogical teachers on the continent. His hour-long talk was packed with good advice and amusing stories. I will pass on a few of his tips.

Use a journal to teach yourself writing. It is not something most of us can do easily to begin with, but if we train ourselves to write a little each day, it becomes a habit. Once we set out to do a project, the small amount we write each day soon builds into something substantial.

If you are having trouble getting going, use a photograph to jump-start the process. This is also a good idea when interviewing relations, who will react to the familiar scenes from their past in the pictures.

Too many of us are waiting to publish once we are 'finished'. Jim told us approvingly that one of his friends entitled his family history, "An Incomplete Genealogy". We should remember that all genealogies are incomplete, because new information (or new babies) are bound to be added later. Whatever you publish, think of it as a work in progress.

If you keep a small notebook with you at all times, you can jot down ideas which come to you while you are driving, eating or on the golf course. Some of us even have our best ideas in the shower (Jim indicated he was one of them). Keep track of those creative concepts and work them up later. Having a notebook full of jottings is also helpful when the time comes to sit down to write. Instead of feeling empty of possibilities, you have a choice of material to write about waiting in the notebook.

Sometimes it can be helpful to have other people to write with. If you know you will be meeting with someone else on a definite date to exchange stories, you are forced to sit down and produce.

Make sure you are comfortable, whether it is at a table, in an easy chair, or in bed. Use the means that you like best too: writing in longhand, a typewriter or a word processor.

If you do want to exchange ideas with someone else, form a writing group of people with similar interests. Meet when you can, exchange experiences and read one another's work. If you have an expert who can 'edit', let them, but it will still be helpful if each one reacts as they wish to the others' writing. Remember what Jim said, however, "If you are going to provide constructive criticism for others, make sure it's the kind you would want to receive yourself."

Writing an entire family history takes a lot of time and effort. Sometimes our families cannot wait that long. Jim told of his Aunt Belle, who was an early enthusiast of his family history project. She shared some information and a few weeks later wanted to know where the family history was. Shown a few family group sheets, she was polite, but still asked where the history was. He eventually wrote two or three pages of basic information, which delighted her. She absorbed them and was ready for more. She told him, "Don't be long, I'm not going to be here forever."

And she wasn't. Jim said she died three weeks before her 103rd birthday.

There is still time to do a little writing project for your family's Christmas stockings. A tiny ten or twenty page book would delight your relations and give you a sense of accomplishment. Then you could say you were no longer "unpublished after all these years."
(17 October 1995)

Quebec Microfilms

An interesting catalogue which I received this week came from La Fédération des Familles-Souches Québécoises. I cannot tell if this is a private or government organization, but their catalogue lists the microfilmed documents available from the National Archives of Quebec which might be useful to genealogists. As well as vast quantities of church records, there are also many notarial records, a prime source for finding marriage and inheritance information in Quebec.

Even if you are not interested in buying microforms, this catalogue is a useful reference tool, as it describes what materials are available in the Archives of Quebec. It could be used to plan research trips in Quebec City.

You can obtain a copy of the catalogue by writing to the Fédération at Case postale 6700, Silléry, Quebec G1T 2W2.

(31 October 1995)

Finding Lost Cousins in New Zealand

Is it possible to find the family of a deceased cousin overseas?

This question came my way from Dr. David Williams of the University of Waterloo. He was demonstrating the use of computers to a group of seniors, and one asked if the World Wide Web could lead to a lost cousin.

In this case, the cousin was from New Zealand. My own Internet expert, Curt Witcher, looked for a suitable net site in the south Pacific. We found a number of interesting possibilities for general information on New Zealand, especially for tourism or business.

For genealogical research in New Zealand, there does seem to be an address which offers a number of different pages. It is http://bitz.co.nz/bitz/explorer.html. Although it turned up many general offerings about genealogy, none of them seemed to be directly connected with this problem.

I turned to the information office at the New Zealand embassy. They did not have many suggestions regarding finding cousins on the Internet, so perhaps (like so much in this new technology), this particular avenue has not developed yet.

They did have other suggestions for the woman with the lost cousins.

You might try finding your cousins through the newspaper. There are two means of doing this.

First, since the cousin you knew died recently, try writing to the local newspaper where she lived to obtain a copy of her obituary. It may contains names and addresses of her next of kin.

Another possibility is to place a small advertisement in the New Zealand newspaper, stating simply who you want to find. They will see it, or one of their friends will.

The national newspaper is the *New Zealand Herald* in Auckland. Its address is Box 32, 46 Albert Street, Auckland; telephone 011 649 379 5050 and fax 011 649 366 0146.

You might have better luck with the local newspaper, however. You can find out what it is and its address by enquiring at the New Zealand High Commission in Ottawa. Their address is 727-99 Bank Street, Ottawa K1P 6G3; telephone (613) 238 5991; fax (613) 238 5707.

If you already know where the family lives, you might try scouring some New Zealand telephone directories. Australian telephone books (and many from other places) are available on the Internet, but not those from New Zealand (as yet). However, paper copies are accessible at the High Commission in Ottawa and they may be willing to look at them for you there.

An interesting source for finding people in New Zealand which is quite different from Canada are the electoral rolls. Everyone who is eligible to vote is required to register there, and these rolls are publicly available. The official I spoke to was unsure if you could consult the whole country's rolls in one place or if you would have to go to the local registry. You can find out by asking the registrar for Wellington. His address is Registrar of Electors, 47 The Esplanade, Petona, Wellington, New Zealand; telephone 011 644 568 9333. This resource is a most valuable one to know about.

While the newspaper sounds like the best possibility, I must say the official I spoke to was helpful and prepared to solve the problem. That famous Kiwi hospitality was very much in evidence.

If anyone else has a similar problem to this woman's, and wishes to locate a cousin or friend in a foreign country, I suggest you start by contacting the embassy for that country in Ottawa. The officials there will suggest the best way to begin your search.

To obtain the address of embassies in Ottawa, call the Kitchener Public Library's Infolink reference service at 743-7502. They also have resources for finding the name and address of newspapers overseas.

(5 December 1995)

Added comment: Use the techniques suggested here to find cousins in any country. Begin by telephoning the embassy in Ottawa to discuss the matter with a knowledgeable official. Telephone calls are more productive than letters A small government of Canada publication lists all the embassies in Ottawa and their personnel. It can be found in most public libraries.

Newspaper Indexes from BurMor

Using newspapers for genealogical research is both rewarding and frustrating. It can also be a lot of hard work.

The rewards are great when you find something. Even a brief item can give us a glimpse into the past when it is written in a quaint style. There can also be colorful detail which we did not know before.

The difficult part is the process which brings us to that tantalizing news item.

First you must determine what newspaper your ancestors regarded as 'local'. This can be surprising.

In early pioneer days, the local paper may have been published many miles away, and in a direction we would not recognize. For example, because of its importance as a milling and transportation centre, Elora was a place that many people visited from northern Wellington county and Grey. Its paper contains many widespread references.

As well, old-time newspapers collected material wherever they could. As a result you can find bits of information miles from where it originated. Only the editor knew how it came to be there.

The best bet is to consider several local newspapers until you begin finding the one which contains your ancestral names.

Then you should determine what issues of that newspaper survive. Nineteenth century newspaper offices seem to have been prone to fire and many are lost. The best resource regarding old newspapers is J. Brian Gilchrist's *Inventory of Ontario newspapers, 1793-1986*. It gives a publishing history, tells what issues are available and where they are. This title is available at the Kitchener library.

Most old newspapers will be accessible on microfilm, following an Ontario universities project to film them two decades ago.

The third stage is actually finding the references to your ancestors. This can be tedious as you wade through years of old newsprint. If you are lucky, someone has done the extracting already.

Craig Burtch of Stratford has spent the past decade doing these extractions for newspapers across southern Ontario. The result is a sizable catalog of booklets.

The best extraction booklets give you the full text of the newspaper items, and an index to see if your names are mentioned. All of Burtch's booklets do this.

To give an interesting example, in a composite booklet of materials from various newspapers of Paris, Galt, Guelph and Ayr, there is a news item from the *Ayr Herald* of May 27, 1867. It describes in great detail the drowning death of David Bowman and the heroic efforts of Theodore Smith to save him.

It continues, "The fur cap of the unfortunate boy floated down the river and was found a few hundred yards below the old distillery, but the body has not yet been found...For a considerable time after the boy fell into the water it was not known to whom he belonged, and a number of parents were exceedingly alarmed lest the child was theirs. The fur cap was of a pattern which many wore and this added to the misery."

This is a graphic image which brings home the tragedy, even to modern minds. For a Bowman or Smith family history, it is an unforgettable story.

Burtch's most extensive extractions include newspapers in Stratford, London, Hamilton, Sarnia and Guelph. He has worked on others as far away as Ottawa, Oshawa and Perth. Even such small papers as the *Atwood Bee* are not neglected.

These booklets are not found as readily in libraries as they should be. However, you may be lucky, especially if you ask for indexes of the local newspaper in the libraries of the area.

The other possibility is to purchase the ones for the town which interests you. They are inexpensive and a fine reference tool.

For details regarding specific newspaper booklets, contact Craig Burtch at Bur-Mor Publications, 359 West Gore, Stratford N5A 1K9. (2 January 1996).

Life Expectancies of Photographs

Photographs are not forever.

Are you surprised? We all think of those hundred year old images we have stored in a closet and think that in another century they will look the same.

This is not necessarily so. Many nineteenth century photographs are yellow and fading. What may be more alarming, colour photos from the 1950s are also on their way out.

A listing of various development processes for pictures indicates how long you can expect them to last:

Black & white negatives	300+ years
Black & white selenium tone print on fiber based paper	200+ years
Cibachrome (from slide)	100+ years
Polacolor II	75+ years
Vericolor II on Ektacolor plus paper	75+ years
Kodachrome 25 & 64 slides	75 to 100 years
Kodachrome II slides	50 years
Video film and movie	30 years
Kodacolor II prints	6 to 10 years
Ektachrome, Agachrome slides	30 years
Kodak instant prints	about 6 months

These times presume that you store the pictures in a dark, cool place. The pictures you hang on the wall or display in frames fade more quickly.

The fact is that the more modern the technology (such as video), the less we know.

It is recommended by experts at Eastman Kodak, the premier film people in the world, that you convert any photos you want to save forever to black and white. What you lose in the immediacy of the colour you will gain in long life.

Those century-old photos that have turned yellow and lost their details can be taken into a photo shop and redone in modern black and white. You will probably find that the details are reborn in the new prints.

Advocates of electronic scanners say that you can do the same by scanning the old pictures onto a disk. This may work if you know exactly what you are doing, and your scanner is a good one. However, scanning technology is in its infancy.

The question of how long pictures will last on computer disk was not addressed in the material which I saw (which was produced by the *Jots from the Point* journal in western Pennsylvania). Perhaps this technology is too new for anyone to judge.

Family historians with extensive genealogical picture collections should make a judgement about which ones they value most. These can be put on disk and printed onto acid-free paper for inclusion in your book history. Even with the state of this technology today, you will ensure that some version of the picture will survive.

Make a negative of the picture in black and white and store it in optimum conditions, carefully labelled. These negatives can be made from prints at most photographic stores.

Perhaps most importantly, make sure copies of your most valued pictures are available to many people in the family. That way, the ones that are lost in fires or moving will not matter. There will be plenty of others that survive.

As for videos, they are one of the most charming of the inventions of the past twenty years. As the success of the television show America's Funniest Home Videos proves, they can capture moments we all want to see again, whether funny or heart-warming.

But remember, no one really knows how long those films will last. And, as technology changes quickly, even if we have the films, we may not have something to show them on.

After all, people made plenty of reel-to-reel tape recordings of family occasions thirty and forty years ago. How can they listen to them now?
(13 February 1996)

How Heavy, How Much, How Long?

Does it seem a long time ago since we measured meat in pounds and distance in miles?

Maybe you never stopped, but children of today have no idea how to use those old measurements. They seem awkward beside the neatness of the metric system.

Our ancestors were used to all the various strange ways of measuring the things around them. If they were British, they not only measured in yards and feet, they weighed in ounces, counted their money in florins, crowns and shillings. People really needed to go to school to find out the long lists of measurements everyone else knew.

Colin R. Chapman, one of the most prominent of English genealogists, has written a short book to tell us more about the ways our ancestors measured. It can serve as a handy reference book when you wade through those ancient documents, diaries or books written in olden times—say before 1960.

He calls the text *How Heavy, How Much and How Long? Weights, Money and Other Measures used by our Ancestors.* One of the forgotten pieces of money recently had a moment in the sun when the European Community was agonizing over what to call its new common currency. Someone suggested reviving the florin, which I last heard of in a Shakespeare play.

It sounded too foreign to Chancellor Kohl and in true bureaucratic fashion, the delegates adopted the euro, a name with no vibrations whatsoever.

Chapman's book reminds us that people made use of what was around them when clarifying early measures. An inch was originally the length of three barleycorns taken from a mature head of barley. Later, Chapman says, someone determined that a barleycorn equaled four poppyseeds.

Most of us who were taught the British system remember that a yard was originally the length from the tip of someone's fingers to their nose. An ell was the same, and used in cloth measurement. Lengths did not stay the same, and an ell gradually became longer than a yard.

A common linear measurement in early Canada was the perch. Early land documents record boundaries as being so many perches, rods or poles from a landmark. These were all the same distance, about 16 and a half feet. Surveyors used the terms because they measured with a pole, and also with chains, which were easy to carry from place to place. Early Canadian deeds also measure distances in chains and links as a result.

There are many more terms that we have totally forgotten. A tuffet is equal to two pecks. The only tuffet I ever knew was the one Little Miss Muffet sat on. In Scotland, small amounts of whiskey can be measured in a mutchkin, which is equal to four gills.

The confusion caused by so many means of measurement could be used to a merchant's advantage. A friend of mine described how his grandmother ran her roadside apple stand using a strange old bucket which she filled with apples and charged for as if it were a peck. If anyone objected, she replied that her family had measured apples in it for generations.

Perhaps it was a tuffet.

Aside from its use as a reference tool, *How Much, How Heavy, and How Long?* will provide a great deal of amusement when we consider those old means by which our ancestors ordered their world. Chapman's lists seem to be endless and include such unusual things as the difference between measuring figs and weighing almonds.

How Much, How Heavy, and How Long? is available from SEL Enterprises, Box 92, Thornhill L3T 3N1.
(27 February 1996)

Preserving Documents

One ongoing question which many genealogists ask has to do with the preservation of family collections. We have papers, photographs, books and family treasures which need special care to last for the future.

Many of the books on this subject are written for professional archivists and do not address the questions in a simple and straightforward way. A new book from Ancestry Inc. in Salt Lake City will help those who want short answers.

A Preservation Guide: Saving the Past and the Present for the Future, by Barbara Sagraves provides sections on paper, books and photographs. There is a brief mention at the end on movies and videotapes, whose lifespan is, as yet, unclear. If you have wondered how to care for your family collection, I can recommend this book as a solution.

A Preservation Guide is available from Ancestry, Inc., Box 476, Salt Lake City UT 84110-0476 USA. For more information, call them at (801) 531-1790.

(2 April 1996)

Current Research in Eastern Europe

Gary Mokotoff is the editor of *Avotaynu* and the foremost North American expert on East European genealogy. He confirms what I have long suspected, that genealogy in the former Iron Curtain countries is on the verge of a big boom.

Many thousands of emigrants came from Eastern Europe to North American in the last two hundred years. In the past twenty years, genealogy has become an interest for many, but those with research interests behind the Iron Curtain could do little. The old Communist governments there did not encourage people from overseas to come and look at their records.

Now things have changed. The prospect of tourist dollars flowing into their needy coffers has encouraged the new governments to begin setting up research bureaux. Mokotoff says that once you make contact with individuals in these countries, you will find them warm and friendly. The difficulty can be determining where to go.

I asked him about the primary problem, which is usually language. If Grandma spoke Polish, but you don't, how can you do research?

Mokotoff insists that it does not need to be an obstacle. Many of the records are tabular in format, so you can learn some basic vocabulary and then begin. Since you will already know the names and places associated with your family, you can look for those.

If you think you have found something but cannot be sure, have someone copy it down for you. Once you get home, you can find a speaker of that language to interpret.

However, Mokotoff says that if you intend to do more extensive research in your ancestral homeland, you should begin by learning the alphabet in use there. After that, some basic skills in the language will come in handy.

I think that you would be well advised to have some language skills. After all, how else will you communicate with those long-lost cousins when you find them?

Archives in Eastern Europe are dissimilar to those we are used to. The original documents may be falling apart from overuse, and most have not been microfilmed or catalogued. You will have the same experiences I had when I began doing my research thirty years ago, before the genealogy boom began.

In those days, we stood in uncomfortable circumstances looking at original documents, dusty, dry and difficult. It was a great deal of fun.

By and large, Mokotoff says, the rule of thumb for finding the documents is this: if they are more than a century old, they will be in a state archives; if less, look in a local archives.

Before venturing overseas, however, you should check the Church of Jesus Christ of Latter-day Saints family history center catalog. A great deal is available on microfilm and more is being filmed every year. Do what research you can in the comfort of home so that you can concentrate on other things once you get there.

Mokotoff's advice is: "You better have the pioneer spirit. If you do, when you get there, you'll be a success."

I asked him to give me a thumbnail sketch of the various countries and their current genealogical resources. The best, he said, were Poland, the Czech Republic, Hungary and Lithuania. Belorus and Ukraine were at a more primitive stage. Merely travelling around in these two countries can be a chore, as there is little gasoline available and many of the archives are in remote towns.

Mokotoff then startled me by saying that Romania was advancing the quickest of them all. I observed that it had been very far behind.

"That's why it's advancing quickest," he replied, "When you start from zero, even being at one is a big step forward."
(16 April 1996)

The Commonwealth War Graves Commission

If someone asked me where Canada's war dead are buried, I would have said France, Holland, Italy, Germany and Hong Kong.

In fact, they are buried in 76 countries around the world. There are 110,000 of them.

The job of caring for the graves falls to the Commonwealth War Graves Commission, based in England but with a Canadian office in Ottawa. The Canadian agency looks after burials in this country and the United States. This involves a surprising 2800 cemeteries in Canada and three memorials to the missing.

The only all-Canadian cemetery is in Sicily.

The graves in Canada are not those of soldiers who died fighting the enemy during the war. Anyone who fell on the battlefield was buried nearby according to the custom of the time. However, many military personnel were lost to disease and accidents here at home, and they might be returned to their native town for burial. In addition there are many foreign soldiers who died and are buried here. The War Graves Commission is also responsible for the prisoners of war buried in Canada, a number of whom rest in Woodland Cemetery in Kitchener.

The policy of the commission is that each individual should be commemorated by a headstone on their grave, or their name on a memorial if their grave is unknown. There is no differentiation by rank, race or creed in the distinctive slab stones.

In the early days of the commission, which was founded after World War I, there were difficulties locating bodies which had been hastily buried on the battlefields. In addition, there was the difficulties that "common soldiers were shoveled into mass graves" while officers were taken home to England by their families.

The current staff of the War Graves Commission have a clear objective to ensure that each dead soldier receives his proper due. This includes inspecting the existing cemeteries and gravestones periodically to ensure they are in good shape. Every site is visited on a rotating basis, even those with only a single burial.

116

Included in their responsibilities are soldiers who died as a result of World War I up to August 1921 (from injuries received) and in World War II up to December 1947. The Korean War and other peacekeeping duties are not included.

The majority of the employees of the War Graves Commission are horticulturalists and stonemasons, who ensure that the cemeteries are well maintained.

The agency in Ottawa employs two officers and clerical staff to answer letters. The headquarters, in Maidenhead, England, has a sizable archives as well as records of all the burials worldwide.

If you have a relative who died in either war and would like to know where they are buried, the War Graves Commission can supply the exact information. This can include a map of the cemetery with the location marked for easy finding if you visit.

In addition, they also have a service which provides photographs of the graves for a nominal fee. If the graves are in a difficult location, you may have to wait until the next inspection visit, but those in the larger cemeteries can be done routinely by staff.

If you have a question for the commission, write to the Canadian agency at 66 Slater Street, Suite 1707, Ottawa K1A 0P4. They ask that you supply the full name, army number and date of death of your relation, or as much detail as you can.

The agency also has a first-rate video about the resting places of Canada's war dead, entitled *Debt of Honor*. It is for sale at $14.00, or can be borrowed from the agency for showing at meetings of interested organizations. Telephone (613) 992-3224 or fax (613) 952-6826 for more information.
(7 May 1996)

Added comment: After writing this column, I asked the War Graves Commission about obtaining a photograph of my great-uncle's grave in France. They set the wheels in motion, but indicated it might take a year or more to arrive. It took three months, and was a first-rate colour picture.

An added surprise was that my great-uncle's file was incomplete. There was no notation that the family had been officially told about the grave (although we had). Since every family has the right to a short, personal inscription on the stone, we can still add something providing the next of kin makes the request.

Two New OGS Guides

The Ontario Genealogical Society has published two new guides which every family historian in the province will need to see.

The more important is a new edition of *Genealogy in Ontario: Searching the Records*, by Brenda Dougall Merriman. It is the basic handbook for Ontario family history. First printed in 1984, it was revised in 1988. This new edition adds a hundred pages of solid and useful information.

Merriman's approach has always been user-friendly. She explains what the records are, where to find them and why you can expect to find the answers in them.

As with the earlier editions, she concentrates on resources available in Toronto, where the Archives of Ontario and the two largest library collections of genealogical books draw most researchers.

An important change has taken place in Ontario research since the 1988 edition. Now, the civil registration records from 1869 to early in this century are available for public scrutiny. Merriman's explanation of this complex topic is clear and helpful for anyone who is coming to the subject for the first time.

Before 1869, there are many possibilities for finding those elusive births, marriages and deaths. Merriman begins with an explanation of pre-1869 vital statistics (for the government did take a disorganized interest in the subject), and then looks at the various alternatives. Her chapter on church records has been greatly expanded to consider how the larger denominations looked at record-keeping in the nineteenth century.

The section on various non-British ethnic groups gives a number of possible places for research, pointing to the recent formation of the Federation of East European Family History Societies and the collections of the Multicultural History Society of Ontario.

In all, this new edition of *Genealogy in Ontario* is an exciting addition to the reference bookshelf. While it will be available in all libraries, most researchers will want to have their own copy at home for constant referrals.

A novel idea is the new book from Althea Douglas of Ottawa. She decided to put together a collection of pointers on trouble-spots in Canadian genealogy. It is called *Here Be Dragons! Navigating the Hazards Found in Canadian Family Research.*

The title comes from a habit common on old maps. When the cartographer did not know what was located in an area, he hid his ignorance with a drawing of a monster and the message: here be dragons!

Her choice of problems is instructive. For example, researchers unfamiliar with the geography of our province might find it confusing that there is a Perth in the west (a county) and another in the east (a town). Douglas explains duplicate and altered names, along with the way land in Canada was divided. There is no common theme to the organization of plots of land, changing from province to province between counties, seigneuries, sections and ranges.

She looks at our British connections in some depth, including military records and the use of honorifics, whether originating in England or in Canada. She laments that it is too bad that British subjects migrating between the homeland, Canada and the other colonies left so few records.

I am happy that Douglas places such an emphasis on geographical knowledge, because she and I agree strongly that knowing the lay of the land is a important step toward finding the information you need.

This charming small book will inform and amuse genealogists across our country. You are sure to learn something from it, as I did.

Genealogy in Ontario: Searching the Records is priced at $29.75 postpaid and including GST. *Here be Dragons!* is $18.00, also including shipping and taxes. They are available from the Ontario Genealogical Society, Suite 102, 40 Orchard View Blvd., Toronto M4R 1B9.
(18 June 1996)

The State Library of Michigan

The State Library of Michigan has many attractions for genealogical researchers.

In the nineteenth century, people in central Ontario with an urge to migrate went west. When they reached Lake Huron, they crossed it and many of them settled in Michigan. As a result, Ontario researchers are often in need of Michigan information.

The State Library and State Archives are in a large complex with the Historical Museum in Lansing, the state capital. The city is an easy four-hour drive from Kitchener, and a pleasant place to visit including the State University of Michigan and a zoo.

The State Library's collection is very large, with an emphasis on family history. Visitors will quickly notice that there are three reference desks in the main reading room, one of them devoted to genealogy. I visited them recently to find details on two branches of my family.

My first interest was to find some obituaries. There is a published newspaper list for the library, much out of date, but current holdings are available in the computer catalogue. I was able to determine which places in Genesee County published newspapers and, using a map, decided which of these was most likely to have published my rural relatives' obituaries.

The microfilmed newspapers are all on self-serve shelving in a special room which includes microfilm readers and printers.

Searching the newspapers for the obituaries reminded me how different papers can be. In Victorian days, every paper seemed to have a column of brief entries for births and deaths. In the early decades of this century, these faded away, and many newspapers had no such announcements. The ones I was looking at fell into this category.

Fortunately the death of my elusive aunt was felt to be newsworthy enough to rate a mention, including confirmation of the old family story that she had emigrated from England on her honeymoon.

The other obituary I needed was easy to locate, since its subject was a civic leader whose sudden death was first-page news.

As I stood by my desk in the reading room wondering what to do next, I was surprised to see a familiar face from Kitchener. Marilyn Baron, an experienced genealogist, has recently discovered the resources of the state library.

She pointed out to me the rows of shelving devoted to individual Michigan counties on the far side of the room. I visited them next and found county histories, indexes, cemetery listings and tax records for Genesee County.

Someone had written down the gravestone inscriptions in the tiny cemetery where my relations are buried, and then annotated them with observations about the individuals involved. This would be very handy for anyone who was at the beginning of their research.

I was surprised to see a new child in the family lineup at this cemetery, Julian F. Heddon. I quickly took the book back to my desk to compare with the family list, and was disappointed to determine that it was a misreading for John R. Heddon. Not all cemetery transcriptions are of the high quality that Norma Huber has provided for Waterloo County.

I found what I was searching for and returned home happy. The genealogical handout for the state library reminds you to do your preparation before you come, know what you want and ask for assistance.

To reach Lansing, take the 401 to the Sarnia cutoff, then the 402 to the border. Once you cross into Port Huron, Michigan, watch carefully, for you are quickly directed to I-69, the southbound expressway. Once you are on I-69, there are no stops until Lansing.

The State Library of Michigan is located at 717 W. Allegan Avenue. Write for information to Box 30007, Lansing MI 48909 USA, or telephone 517-373-1580.

(2 July 1996)

British Local and Family History

We all know the value of a dictionary.

When you need to know something quickly and easily, a dictionary is the place to turn. Usually, we think of language books and the old schoolroom command: Look it up in the dictionary!

Most genealogists know that there are other kinds of dictionaries which can be helpful. For those with British interests, the new *Oxford Companion to Local and Family History*, by David Hey, will provide many resources for both quick and in-depth answers.

Our shared language and culture sometimes blind us to the fact that Britain is a foreign country. So many of the ways of doing things are different there, and hard to understand. If we hear a reference to a 'carrier', we think of disease. The English envisage a loaded wagon.

The church calendar made itself felt in everyday life there more than here. Few Canadians would know when Lady Day was, or the time of Lammas grazing.

Lady Day (March 25) was the first day of the year until 1752 in England and Wales. The English have always divided the year into quarters, on the 25th of March, June, September and December. Rents and other monies were traditionally paid on those days.

Lammas grazing took place on 1 August until 1752, 13 August afterward. Lammastide was the middle of the harvest period.

Brief and useful explanations of phrases such as this are one of the advantages of Hey's *Companion*. I can warn you: if you pick it up for a quick look at one thing, you are bound to be attracted to another entry nearby, and you will end up browsing for hours.

Hey tells us that ducks were fattened in East Anglia for sale in London 'in the early modern period', but not as many as geese and turkeys. Norfolk turkeys were so famous, they are still considered the best kind to buy for an English Christmas.

The amazing thing is that flocks of both turkeys and geese were driven to market. Imagine seeing an English road in December, with hundreds of fowl calmly marching to their doom.

Hey cross-references the many linked articles in the *Companion*, to ensure readers find as much information as possible. The brief paragraph on orphans, for example, refers also to poor apprentices, factory owners (presumably wicked ones), foundlings, the poor law, record offices, Dr. Barnardo's and the Court of Ward and Liveries.

The Barnardo entry is brief and dry, but does remind people that the orphanage, one of Britain's largest, had the unusual policy of photographing all its charges. The photographic archive contains 55,000 pictures and it is possible for descendants of the Barnardo orphans to obtain copies of their ancestor's likeness. The *Companion* gives the title of a magazine article which will explain how.

Readers of historical novels will recognize references to a dovecote. Few houses have them here, but they were once common, to house pigeons. Hey says, "Pigeons were valued for their meat, eggs, feathers, down and dung." I wondered what the pigeon feathers were used for, because it was considered bad luck to use them in pillows, guaranteeing bad dreams.

This is probably a good suggestion for a birthday or Christmas present, because it's costly ($66.95) but once you have it, the *Companion* will remain a treasured part of your reference library as long as you are interested in English research. I will keep my copy alongside Pauline Saul's *The Family Historian's Enquire Within* and my list of local registry offices.

The Oxford Companion to Local and Family History, by David Hey, is published by Oxford University Press Canada. It is available from your favourite bookstore.
(6 August 1996)

Erie Canal

The annual conference of the Federation of Genealogical Societies was held in Rochester, N.Y. this year. If you look at the country between K-W and Rochester on a map, you would never guess that the American city played a vital role in the early history of this area.

When the first wave of German immigrants headed for Waterloo County in the 1820s, they had a difficult time finding their way. Most of them lived near the Rhine and had to make the long journey downriver to Holland or overland to France. Their voyage across the Atlantic brought them to the United States, because there were no direct sailings to Canada.

Although some of them went to Baltimore or Philadelphia, the majority landed in New York. From there they headed up the Hudson River north to Canada.

They were lucky. The Erie Canal had recently been completed and offered two easy routes to Canada and the German-speaking county where they wanted to settle.

The Erie Canal has been described as the American nation's "greatest non-military accomplishment." When it was first proposed to build a canal which would link the Hudson River with Lakes Ontario and Erie, conservative politicians said it could not be done. The idea was too large for many imaginations.

However, the visionaries in the New York government pushed it through. The canal was begun in 1817 and finished in 1825, linking the river first with Buffalo and then on a northern spur with Rochester.

The canal meant that it was possible to sail the 425 miles from New York City to Buffalo during the fine weather months. The ease of travel was remarkable in a day when roads were mostly muddy trails pitted with stumps and holes.

The canal closed during the winter, but if immigrants were only partway on their journey, they could stop for a time at one of the cities along the way. This accounts for the occasional baby in Waterloo County families who lists New York State as a birthplace.

The result of the canal's opening was immediate. Before, Buffalo had been a village and Rochester an unimportant port. Almost at once, Buffalo became an important industrial centre.

Rochester's fame was founded on its mills, which encouraged the growth of grain farms nearby. Many of the German immigrants who intended to settle in Waterloo County stopped here and never finished the trip.

The canal was very busy, with "unbroken lines of boats moving in either direction." People who were uneasy with innovation found the speed of travel on the canal to be unsafe. One man described his trip "rocketing across the state at four miles an hour."

Immigrants heading for K-W had a choice. Those who went to Buffalo could cross the Niagara River and then continue overland. Rufus Sattler, whose leather-goods store on Queen Street South was a landmark for decades, told how his emigrant ancestor reached Buffalo with only twenty-five cents in his pocket. He set out on foot for Berlin (as Kitchener was then called).

Through the kindness of farmers met along the way, he arrived in town with his twenty-five cents intact.

Immigrants from Rochester took the ferry to Hamilton. They could also sail to Toronto or Belleville across the lake. From Hamilton they had the old Dundas road as a starting point for their journey through Galt to Berlin.

The Erie Canal is credited with helping to open the old American western trail to Ohio and Michigan. It is interesting to realise that it also contributed to the development of our own area.

If you wish to know more about the history of the Erie Canal, the Rochester Public Library recommends *Stars in the Water*, by George Condon (1974), from which the quotations in this column are taken.

(3 September 1996)

How to Learn through Tapes and Lectures

Genealogical researchers have a lot of learning to do.

You may think that it is simple to sit down with the available resources and come up with the facts on your family. Almost certainly you will miss some details if you do not understand the background involved.

For example, words change their meanings over the years. An old will may refer to someone as a "brother-in-law." We know what that means, don't we? Well, a century or more ago, it might have meant "stepbrother." Even today, I hear people refer to someone as a "stepbrother" when I know they mean "half-brother."

And in our sensitive society, it is sometimes considered ill-mannered even to mention that someone is a step-sibling or only half-related. We say simply "brother" and everyone is happier. Who knows what generations in the future will think of that.

In his entertaining and informative lecture "When one record is wrong, but you don't know which one", Henry Hoff of New York presented this problem, and a variety of others with advice on their solutions. He wisely counselled every researcher to examine all documents thoroughly before making a decision. If there is a difference between originals, you must consider the sources and make an informed judgement.

Hoff reminded us that most of our ancestors were illiterate, and the documents relating to them were dictated to someone else: census takers, registry clerks, clergy. It is quite possible that the names are not merely spelled wrong, but mixed up completely. What about William R. Buckle, for

124

instance. He would not appear in an index under A (for Arbuckle) as you might expect.

Thomas Seldon might become Thomas Eldon. All of the various name prefixes (Fitz, Mac, De, Van and Von) come and go according to the weather or the whims of the moment. The ends of names also vary, with Stevenson becoming Stevens.

Hoff recommends always saying the names you see aloud. If it sounds like the name you are searching for, it may well be the one.

Not all the errors caused by dictated documents are the fault of the clerk. My own great-grandfather was born in Lancashire and had a healthy brogue all his life. He would celebrate the birth of each of his children before going to the registry office, and the result was occasional confusion. The fact that he had a daughter Marion in 1901 seems to have slipped his mind in 1906, when another daughter (meant to be called Marjorie) was also registered as Marion. The error was not discovered for several decades.

Hoff has two practical solutions for those trying to sort out discrepancies of this sort.

First, he suggests setting aside one of the documents and then comparing all the others. Do this with different documents in the 'isolated' position until you see which of them doesn't belong.

The other possibility is to set the whole problem aside for a while. When you come back to it later, you will have a fresh viewpoint and be in a better position to make a judgement.

You might also put the question to someone who has never seen it before, and whose opinion you trust. Once again, a fresh viewpoint might help solve the matter.

Difficult questions may be frustrating, but the detective work they require is what makes genealogy such a rewarding activity.

Henry Hoff gave his lecture at the Federation of Genealogical Societies conference in Rochester. Tapes of this and other lectures from the conference can be purchased from Repeat Performance, 2911 Crabapple Lane, Hobart IN USA 46342. For a complete price list, phone (219) 947-1024.

(15 October 1996)

More: Repeat Performance has an extensive catalogue of taped lectures from Federation of Genealogical Societies and National Genealogical Society conferences in the United States. Although you may not be interested in the geographically-specific American talks, the methodology lectures may be very useful. The speakers are among the most distinguished on the continent. The Ontario Genealogical Society has begun the practice of taping its Seminar lectures too; enquire for available tapes at the OGS office.

Resources at the Glenbow Museum in Calgary

When I left for Calgary, a friend told me that the Glenbow Museum had a herd of buffalo at its back door, to demonstrate the way things used to be on the prairies. As my taxi pulled up in front of a skyscraper in downtown Calgary, I doubted it.

Three floors of the building house the museum exhibits, which currently include the Alberta Biennale, the latest in the province's paintings, galleries which show how the pioneers lived and some mouth-watering cases of Medalta porcelain, made in Medicine Hat.

The floor above that will be your aim if you are a genealogical researcher. It houses both the library and archives, rich in resources concerning the three prairie provinces. The public is welcome.

The library's collection contains materials from Manitoba to the Rockies, with an emphasis on southern Alberta. They have a very large collection of local histories of the province. Nowadays, these tend to be huge and heavy volumes containing many family histories as well as local stories, so they are invaluable for genealogists.

One of their programs is a clipping and indexing file of Calgary newspapers that goes back to 1883. Lindsay Moyer, the librarian in charge, says that now they try to cover all possible subjects but the earlier indexes may have been more selective. "You know how old-time librarians were," she says, "At one time, we had fat files on the Anglicans and nothing on the Catholics."

There are also published indexes from Lethbridge and Fort Macleod newspapers.

The library maintains a periodical index, more intensive on local subjects than the published indexes.

The library's catalogue is mostly in the computer now, with more being added all the time. At the other end of the room, the Glenbow Archives also has an online database covering its manuscript collections. The text-based system means that individual names which appear in the manuscripts can be searched, opening the door for quick and intensive work by researchers.

For those with Métis ancestry, the Denney collection offers wide possibilities for research. It is indexed in the Archives' files. The Denney

126

materials are now on microfilm and can be borrowed on interlibrary loan. Also available on loan are the Treaty Pay Lists, which include every member of aboriginal families who were eligible and cover the 1870-1890 period.

Nationally-known Métis genealogical expert Geoff Burtonshaw visits the Archives several times a month to assist researchers. His schedule is posted by the elevator so you can plan to be there when he is.

The library has many regional directories going back to 1884 (which include all the old North-West), city directories from Manitoba to British Columbia, homestead records, cemeteries and telephone directories for Alberta. Tax records for Calgary are at the City of Calgary Archives close by, and again freely available to the public. Although the Calgary Public Library is also nearby, researchers might be advised to head for the Glenbow first.

Researchers who have Alberta connections will find a visit to the Glenbow Museum library and archives a fruitful research trip. As always with long-distance research, write ahead to make sure what you want is available, and plan your work carefully. You can be sure of a warm welcome at the Glenbow and working at the old oaken desks there is a pleasure.

The Glenbow Museum is at 130 - 9 Avenue SE, Calgary T2G 0P3. Phone the library at (403) 268-4197 and the Archives at (403) 268-4204. Their joint fax is (403) 232-6569.

As for buffalo, they do have two. They are stuffed, of course, and a sign beside them reads, "Please do not touch Ethel."
(5 November 1996)
More: Researchers needing help in Calgary and Edmonton should look at the handbook Tracing Your Ancestors in Alberta: A Guide to Sources of Genealogical Interest in Alberta's Archives an d Research Centres, *by Victoria Lemieux and David Leonard. It is available from genealogical booksellers or from the publishers Lemieux/Leonard Research Associates, 9809-85 Avenue, Edmonton AB T6E 2J5. A column on Edmonton appeared on 6 May 1997 (see below).*

Reading the Census

Have you ever wondered what it was like when the old-time census taker came to the door?

You should, if you want to understand the census records which your family left behind.

I usually tell researchers that the census should be their first port of call when they begin gathering data about their families. There are six Ontario census' available (1851, 1861, 1871, 1881, 1891, 1901), one of which (1871) has been completely indexed.

The information available in the census will provide a picture of your family over fifty years, with approximate birthdates, places of birth, occupations and relationships.

But the real question is: how trustworthy is it? And having told you it is indispensable, I can say that the answer to that question is, not very.

The census taker was a political appointee, given the job for his loyalty to his party and not for his spelling abilities. He travelled from house to house in his buggy, stopping and questioning whoever was home about the inhabitants. He wrote down the answers as they were given.

Here we find the first problem. He may have been speaking to an adult who knew about the family, but he may also have been talking to one of the children. Or a visitor. Their knowledge of Mother's age or Father's place of birth may have been doubtful.

The speaker may also have been illiterate, as a good percentage of the population was in those days. They gave the names of the family members in their own way (perhaps with a strong Donegal or Bavarian accent). The census taker wrote them down as he heard them.

The task for modern researchers is to decipher our family's name from what he wrote. Agnes Lon and her family, in the 1871 census of Durham county, are in fact, Lunn. If you say Lunn with a Belfast accent (as many of the family still do, in the sixth generation in Canada), you get Lon.

People's ages often do not advance in ten-year increments, because they never had to write them down any other time. Many of them had only the vaguest idea of their correct age or birthdate. And invariably there were those who changed their age to suit circumstances.

The advantage of having six census' to look at, is that if you have six answers to the age question, you do get a general picture of when that person was born. And in the case of 1901, you get an exact birthday to work with as well.

The 1901 census also offers the year of emigration for those born outside Canada.

What about those whose names changed? Keep in mind nineteenth century naming customs, which equated Ann with Nancy, and Mary with Polly. Also remember that the German custom of using the last given name clashes with the English habit of using the first. A German speaker may have announced a name as "Katharina Margaretha Hoffman", knowing that the woman was called "Margaretha" by her friends. The English census taker would have recorded her as "Katharina M. Hoffman" or even "Catherine Hoffman." Would you recognize your Margaret if you saw this name on the census list?

I recommend making copies of all the census entries for your family, amalgamating the information and using it wisely. Every couple of years, go back and look at the originals again. The experience you have gained in your research may help you re-interpret the data you see there.

And by the way, the last time I wrote about the census in this column, an official from Statistics Canada wrote me a warning letter telling me I should never again suggest that the 1911 census would ever be available to the public. He said it never will.

But then, Statistics Canada said the same thing about the 1901 census ten years ago, and look where it is now.
(19 November 1996)

A Discovery in Tillsonburg

A letter I received recently contained an idea for a new genealogical technique.

Donald S. Walker, now of Middlebury, Connecticut, was born in Tillsonburg in 1924. His mother died in 1926 and his father moved to the United States, leaving him with his grandparents. In 1929, his father married again, reclaimed his son, and Mr. Walker's ties with Canada were broken.

In retirement he found himself living among some genealogists. Not surprisingly, he became interested in his own roots. As I have often observed, interest in family history is catching.

By joining his local genealogical society and the Oxford County branch of the Ontario Genealogical Society, he found himself able to obtain resources to trace his father's family to his satisfaction. However, he knew very little about his mother's relations and did not feel able to proceed.

He decided to make a return visit to Tillsonburg, hoping to find someone who could help him. Very wisely, he made extensive preparations before the trip.

His aim was to find someone who had known his mother's family, and could give him some tips on where to look next. Since the names he knew lived

129

there a long time ago, he knew he would have to consult elderly residents of the town.

He obtained a list of nursing and residential care homes in the area, and wrote letters to the administrators of each. He told them his objective, and asked them for names of persons he might interview. He also made it clear that if they had any objection to his visiting their facility, they could simply say so and he would not bother them.

At the first place he visited, he talked to several people, all of whom suggested he see the same man, a well-known historian in the town.

At the second place, he hit gold. He found a woman who had known the family, and was even a very
distant relation. She could not give him much concrete information, but suggested that he get in touch with another woman, who lived in a nearby town. When he did so, he found that she was his first cousin. "We always wondered what happened to you," she said.

Mr. Walker's good idea certainly paid off. He not only approached his idea with imagination, he organised the search in a sensible way.

I have often helped individuals searching for lost relations by asking their former neighbours if they know where family members are living today. Once I was able to link a Hamilton man with a daughter in England whom he had never seen, the product of a wartime romance. A former neighbour provided the necessary information.

Genealogists certainly cannot begin randomly prowling the halls of care facilities in the hope of finding someone to help with their research. We can keep in mind that there may be people who knew our relatives. Mr. Walker's technique of beginning by asking permission and suggestions of the facility administrator is a good one.

Also remember that many people in care facilities have few visitors and will enjoy talking about the past, even with a stranger. Every senior citizens' home is a goldmine of information about the past of their community.

And for those of you who have interests in Tillsonburg, the library there publishes *The Tillsonburg Public Library Genealogy Index*. It is a multi-volume work which now covers 1863-1935.

Bur-Mor in Stratford has published extracts from the *Tillsonburg Observer* for 1863-1872, and NorSim Publishing in Delhi includes St. Paul's United Church marriages 1896-1902 in one of its publications.

Two histories of the town, *Tillsonburg a History*, and *Early Tillsonburg*, both by John Irwin Cooper,will help fill in the background.
(3 December 1996)

Martha's Christmas Celebration

My friend Martha Barnhart had an original idea for enhancing her family's Christmas celebration.

In the hurly-burly of Christmas Day, we may be too busy to stop and actually enjoy what is happening. Our modern lives are full of hurried activity and we seldom slow down to reflect on what we are doing.

Martha's idea encouraged her family to consider their feelings about Christmases past.

As their Christmas dinner came to an end, Martha disappeared for a moment and then came back with a box brimming with small gifts.

There was one gift for each person at the table. I should tell you that Martha's Christmas parties are large, upwards of twenty people.

To earn their gifts, Martha told them, each person would have to contribute a favourite Christmas memory. Realizing that some people may have been shy about talking to the group, Martha began the storytelling herself. Then she looked around the table for the next volunteer.

The gifts she had chosen were small tokens, but selected with their recipient in mind. The group at the dinner consisted of four generations of Martha's family and included friends as well as relations.

The stories were varied, some of them simple and some more elaborate. The youngest person there was less than two years old, so his story was told by a grandparent, and described the previous Christmas, the only other Yuletide he had experienced.

One or two of the participants were quite shy when their turn came, but the spirit of the day prevailed.

This kind of creativity helps to make a special day even better, by focusing on what we love most about this season. Martha recorded the stories as they were told, and then wrote them down. They have become a chapter in her autobiography, which she is giving her family as a present next week. In effect, she created a Christmas memory simply by having people tell some of their best experiences.

Rather than let your Christmas whiz by in a blur of meaningless activity, stop for a moment and remember. Record the best of Christmas memories for your family's history.

(17 December 1996)

Baptismal Records

People looking for ancestors in the early nineteenth century often say, "I am looking for their birth certificate." They are unlikely to find one.

Before government registration of births began in Ontario in 1869, there was no such thing as a 'birth certificate.' It is possible to find the birthdate of someone born then. Perhaps a family member wrote it down somewhere, often in a bible. Age and birthday are stated on the 1901 census, and a quick calculation will give a birthdate.

But for most people, we will never know their exact date of birth. The alternative is a baptismal date.

Most children in early Canada were baptised (or christened) because this was a routine custom of their parents. Most people were Roman Catholics, Anglicans, Presbyterians or Methodists, all of whom practised infant baptism.

What this custom meant and how we can use these records to reckon our ancestors' ages from them are explained in John T. Humphrey's new book, *Understanding and Using Baptismal Records.*

In earlier days, babies were hurried to the font by parents who feared their early death. If the child were unbaptised, they could not be buried in consecrated ground and their souls would be in danger in the next world. In Roman Catholic countries, in particular, the custom of quick baptism continued for a long time.

Presbyterians and Methodists took their time making christening arrangements. In colonial Canada, the process was made more difficult because the circuit-riding clergyman stopped by only every few weeks or months. Some parents were so neglectful, they saved up a quiverful of children for a mass baptising every five or ten years! These lists of children all with the same parents and a common baptismal date, are the cause of much grief to researchers trying to sort them out by birth year.

One of my more difficult ancestors has no baptismal record that I can find. However, he must have been to the font at some point, for we find a little note after the record of his brother's christening, "Received into the church at the same time, his brother John Payne Hewitt also." He would have been about ten then, but the circumstances remain a mystery.

Humphrey's approach is historical, outlining the theological basis for infant baptism (which every genealogist should understand). He then tells us what the various sects believed, so we can tell what our ancestors were doing. Each seems to have had their own approach to the question, which resulted in differing forms of records.

The chapter called "Evaluating the Evidence" is very useful. Using Pennsylvania as his example, Humphrey describes changing attitudes toward baptismal practice and record-keeping. From this, genealogists will discover new strategies for finding their own family's records.

My colleague John Beatty suggested that there were too many Pennsylvania references in the book. This state is Humphrey's area of expertise, but the examples can, in the reader's imagination, be expanded to cover any geographical area. Religious ideas before 1900 may have originated anywhere in Europe or North America, but the printed word ensured they spread quickly. The schism in the Church of Scotland took only a few weeks to spread to Ontario in the 1840s, despite the slowness of transportation across the Atlantic.

This brief book will take only an afternoon to read, but is sure to educate both beginners and experienced researchers. I will certainly want a copy for my own reference shelf.

Understanding and Using Baptismal Records is available from the author, John T. Humphrey, at Box 15190, Washington DC USA 20003.
(7 January 1997)
The current price of this book is US$17.95. When ordering by mail, add a suitable amount for postage. It can also be found at general genealogical booksellers.

The Saskatchewan Residents Index

Imagine an index that lists everyone who ever lived in a place. One glance, and you could tell if your family member was there.

The Saskatchewan Genealogical Society has set out to do this for its province. The Saskatchewan Residents Index (SRI) gathers references to individuals from various kinds of historical resources and lists them alphabetically. The database, which is available at the SGS offices in Regina, will quickly narrow down the possibilities for researchers who have lost someone in Saskatchewan.

Aside from homesteaders who spent a lifetime in the west, many Canadians spent brief periods of time in the prairie provinces during the early days. Men who were looking for work could take special trains west at harvest time to help bring in the grain. Many of these men might have stayed for a few months or years. Others tried prairie life and found it too difficult, so they returned to Ontario.

The SRI was first suggested as a way of celebrating the SGS' 25th anniversary in 1994. Although everyone knew "this was going to be a monster", they began indexing in 1990, using only family names.

As the index grew, they realized that family names were not enough. "What can you do with a thousand Smiths?" points out Marge Thomas, executive director of SGS.

So they scrapped what they had and started again, this time indexing persons. As well as their names, the index locates them in a specific place and time, gives the source of the information and where you can access the material. At a time when most indexes tend to be too brief, this one seems to have considered everything you will need to know.

Thomas says that SGS is concentrating on local histories. "Saskatchewan has lots of these," she points out. Thomas estimates that newer local histories run from 400 to a thousand pages each. Most contain family histories.

In addition to local histories, the index includes archival files of various kinds, government documents, maps and newspaper indexes. By 'government documents', they mean such things as enumerators' lists. Currently, SGS is adding its collection of cemetery inscriptions to the SRI.

SGS has a network of volunteers to keep SRI growing. Every entry is verified and then re-checked to ensure accuracy.

The initial data entry is done by people at home. Some work on disk, but some transcribe by hand and the data entry is done by someone else. The toughest job is extracting the material. Thomas says that some volunteers reckon that it takes five hundred hours to index one of those huge local histories.

Currently the index has more than 1,100,000 names. To consult it in person costs $1 per name for members, $2 for non-members. If you are not going to be in Regina, you can have SGS do it for you, at a cost of $3 for three pages of printout (members) or $6 (non-members). Considering the labour involved, this is remarkably inexpensive.

SGS is a going concern, with offices and a library at 1870 Lorne Street, Room 201, in Regina and twenty-five branches spread around the province. Although many of them are very small, they represent contacts which might help you to find your Saskatchewan connections. For a list of the branches and their addresses, look at the December 1996 issue of the SGS Bulletin, available at the Kitchener Public Library.

To enquire about using the SRI in person or by mail, you can write to SGS at Box 1894, Regina SK S4P 3E1. Telephone to (306) 780-9207 or fax (306) 781-6021. More information about their activities, including the SRI, can be found at their website: http://www.regina.ism.ca/orgs/sgs/index.htm. (4 February 1997)

More: The SGS website includes access to their library catalogue (so you can find out what they have from the comfort of your own computer) and a separate area for the personal home pages of SGS members. One of them may live in your family's home town.

The huge local histories which Marge Thomas mentions are now common in Manitoba and Alberta as well as Saskatchewan. The nearest libraries to southwestern Ontario which own large collections of these are the National Library of Canada, Ottawa (website at http://www.nlc-bnc.ca) and the Allen County Public Library, Fort Wayne, Indiana (website at http://www.acpl.lib.in.us). You can check their catalogues from home on the Internet and then consider a visit to look at the giant volumes which interest you.

The Society of Genealogists, London, England

Imagine working in a genealogical library for more than forty years.

Anthony Camp, current director of the Society of Genealogists in London, England, has been with the society for that long. I was pleased to have a chance to talk to him about the Society when I was passing through London, especially as he has announced that he will retire at the end of 1996.

The Society of Genealogists was founded in 1911. It has been in its current building in east London since 1984, and is already bursting at the seams. There are three floors of library shelves, with a classroom and lounge in the basement. The main floor contains offices and a fine bookshop.

The society publishes *The Genealogist's Magazine*, a quarterly. Members have access to the library, which is one of the largest of its kind in Britain. They are currently converting their card catalogue to a computer database, using lottery funding. They have also recently acquired a FamilySearch station which provides data from Salt Lake City available on CD-ROM.

Camp points out that the English section of the International Genealogical Index, an important part of FamilySearch, is better than for other countries, because the LDS volunteers have done more microfilming there than elsewhere. Very little filming is going on now, which is unhappy news for those of us who hope that the significant gaps in the IGI English entries will be filled.

The library is arranged geographically. The bindings in each section are colour-coded so that cemeteries, church records, and census are all immediately identifiable.

The Society of Genealogists' library accepts all donated materials offered to it, whether (as Camp says) they are on the back of an old envelope or in the margins of a copy of *War and Peace*. The books go directly on the shelf, while the lesser offerings are placed in special files alphabetically by family name.

The Society's files are extensive, and have been available in their paper format on the shelves. Some of them are rather tattered after years of use, so the Society is currently converting the loose paper files into microfiche. This way, they have a longer lifespan and take up less space. The original papers are being put into storage.

Since the index to the 1881 English and Welsh census has been completed, a new large project was needed. This is the National Burials Index Project. It is beginning by indexing parish registers from 1812-1837, ending when civil registration began. 1812 was chosen as a starting date because new record forms were used by the Church of England beginning in that year. They are the most easily read parish records up to that time.

The National Burials Index Project will serve as an adjunct to the IGI, which does not include death records. The collecting of the data has recently begun, so no decision has yet been made about how the index will be published. Camp thinks that microfiche is the ideal format, but perhaps CD-ROM is more likely, because completeness will be emphasized.

Researchers with English roots who are visiting London are welcome to use the society's library, on payment of a fee. The Society can be found north of Barbican underground station. It is a little difficult to see, so it is best to obtain clear directions from the Society before travelling.

Anyone who has ongoing interests in England may want to join. The Society now has 14,000 members and is growing steadily. The current cost is £21.00 per year.

Write for a brochure (including an addressed envelope and sufficient British postage or two International Reply Coupons) to Society of Gene-

alogists, 14 Charterhouse Buildings, Goswell Road, London EC1M 7BA England. The Society does not undertake research.
(18 March 1997)

The Society of Genealogists' Bookshop

Imagine standing in a bookstore that offers several hundred titles on British genealogy, and nothing else.

If you have research interests in this area, it's like being a child in a candy store. I felt that way in the Society of Genealogists shop in London a few weeks ago.

There were the two books on English research which I think everyone should keep close by. One is Pauline Saul's *The Family Historian's Enquire Within* (5th ed.) and the other Colin Rogers' *The Family Tree Detective*. Saul's book is a dictionary-style reference tool for resources and concepts in British genealogy. Rogers looks at genealogical problems and gives strategies to solve them using a clearly designed path, something like a flow chart.

Rogers has a new book, *The Surname Detective*, which looks at family names, how and where they occur and why.

British genealogists are familiar with the several series of small booklets, each offering information on one subject. The best known of these are the Gibson Guides, all co-written and edited by Jeremy Gibson.

The Gibson Guides tend to look at one topic and describe where to find that kind of resource throughout England. Using them, you can ask, "Where can I find voters' lists in Leicestershire?" or "Are there militia records for Somerset?" and find exactly where to look. I bought lists of coroners' records, census and newspaper indexes, tax assessments and local court records. The latter are particularly useful for finding the parents of illegitimate children.

Experienced researchers may be familiar with the McLaughlin Guides (by Eve McLaughlin), which summarized one topic each. These are going out of print, but the Federation of Family History Societies have started a new series to replace them. They are called "*An Introduction to....*" I bought the ones on deeds, occupations, wills and probate, newspapers and the British Army. Military records are crammed with juicy information, but finding your ancestor in the first place can be difficult. Iain Swinnerton's booklet on the army looks very helpful.

The Society of Genealogists itself has two series of good resource guides. One looks at items in their own library and offers help in finding what you need. Looking at these will probably send you straight to the airport with tickets for London.

They have lists of parish register copies (for 16,000 parishes), directories and voters' lists, will indexes, and instructions on how to use some special collections which are located there, such as *Boyd's Marriage Index*. As Boyd's is also available through the LDS family history centers, the guide can be useful right here at home.

The Society's other series of booklets explains how to access resources on specific topics. Some are general, such as the booklets on Scotland and railway employees. Others look at non-Anglican religious groups, whose records may be hard to find. I picked up guides for Baptists, Congregationalists, Jews and the Salvation Army.

There are also plenty of county genealogical guides. I found quite a variety, including Cambridgeshire, Lancashire, Northampton, Norfolk, Bedford, the Isle of Man, Yorkshire, two on Gloucestershire. Scotland is included, with Strathclyde and "North East Roots" which covers Elgin, Aberdeen, Banff and Grampian.

I would need much more space to cover everything. If you would like a list of what they sell, write to the Society of Genealogists at 14 Charterhouse Buildings, Goswell Road, London EC1M 7BA England enclosing a stamped self-addressed envelope (British stamps or international reply coupons). They sell books by mail.

Many of the books on sale in London can be purchased in Canada through SEL Enterprises, Box 92, Thornhill ON L3T 3N1. Include a long stamped envelope if you write to them, too.

(15 April 1997)

The Edmonton City Archives

What do you do if you have an empty drill hall and no soldiers to march in it?

You might very well build an archives inside. That's what Edmonton did. The result is a city's history on display in a safe and modern setting.

The Edmonton archives was founded in 1938. It lived in cramped quarters until the federal government vacated the huge drill hall in the north end. A creative architect built a smaller building inside, and this is where the archives now sits. Every space is roomy, with plenty of area for expansion.

138

Since the archives has so much extra space, they rent out the spare rooms to various heritage groups, including the Alberta Genealogical Society. There are enough meeting rooms for a large conference there, too.

The archives' first purpose is to house city government documents under a records policy formulated in 1971. However, anything on paper about Edmonton is welcome, and the city archivist makes a point of being flexible when he is offered materials. There is another center for artifacts.

The archives does not think of itself as a first stop for family researchers, but can "flesh out what the genealogists already have." It actively cooperates with the Alberta Provincial Archives, and Edmonton Public Library is providing research materials for genealogists.

There are maps of the city dating back to its earliest days, telephone books and Henderson directories from 1899 to the present. The directory collection is incomplete.

The city's tax records are on file here, and they may be one of the most important collections from a genealogical point of view. This includes the List of Burgesses (or landowners).

The archives also owns 45,000 cataloged photographs, and another 100,000 uncataloged ones. These are still available to those who want to look, but not as easily found. The photographic index, which I saw, is very easy to use and includes a copy of the picture.

Visitors can also consult the Archives Network of Alberta in computer form. This is a cooperative effort by 23 institutions throughout the province, which provides descriptive access to more than 500 manuscript collections. If the material you want is not in Edmonton, you can find out where it is and how to access it elsewhere.

The collection contains other materials which might surprise you, such as a much valued collection of material from Amber Valley in the Athabaska region. It concerns African-American families from Texas and Oklahoma who moved to Alberta at the turn of the century. Their story is an unusual one.

Why is this material found at the Edmonton City Archives? Because while the archives has a legal responsibility to own certain government documents, the archivists are also aware of the 'enduring value' of other materials which might be in search of a home. The Edmonton archives will supply it.

Your relations in the Edmonton area may well show up in the extensive finding aids collection here. You can visit the archives at 10440 -

108 Avenue Edmonton AB T5H 3Z9, or telephone (403) 496-8710. On the Internet, look at www.gov.edmonton.ab.ca/parkrec/archives.
(6 May 1997)
More: For information on the genealogical handbook for Alberta, look at the column about the Glenbow Museum (5 November 1996), above.

Medical Records at the Archives of Ontario

Medical records can provide an interesting glimpse into our relations' lives. They can also prove—or discredit—family legends.

At the recent Ontario Genealogical Society Seminar, Carolyn Heald of the Archives of Ontario discussed medical records in her care there.

Many people look for hospital records at the archives, but they will be disappointed. Hospitals are not government institutions, and have no responsibility for keeping their documents or making them public.

Doctors' records can be found there, however. These are often account books, with single pages indicating the amounts owed by one family. It is possible to use these records to follow the course of an illness, although the information given is slight. If you are lucky, a more detailed journal may be included.

These records come from all over, and are in the Archives of Ontario by chance. There is a published guide, which is available in the Reading Room. If you do not find a local doctor there, check in archives which are closer to where your family lived.

Heald told how the true story of the death of Susannah Doner in 1872 was revealed by her doctor's journal. The story was that she had been jilted and died of a broken heart. The doctor's records revealed she had an illegitimate child, which caused her to leave her parents' house. She died of complications from the delivery, and the fate of the baby is not known.

Heald also mentioned that obstetrical details of the births of children, particularly difficult births, may be found in these records. These will be of great interest to anyone compiling a medical family tree.

Quite substantial records can be found at the Archives for psychiatric hospitals and tuberculosis sanatoria, both of which are run by the provincial government.

Records for the Queen Street Hospital in Toronto go back to its beginnings in 1839. There are nineteenth century records for the institutions in London, Hamilton and Kingston and from Penetang from 1904.

These records largely consist of death and discharge records, admissions and case logs. As you might guess, it is possible for some of them to be lengthy and detailed.

These documents are governed by the Freedom of Information Act and the Mental Health Act. If you have a relative who spent time in one of these hospitals, you should begin by looking at these two acts to determine what records might be made available to you, and under what circumstances. Copies of all provincial acts can be found in the reference department of the Kitchener library.

For those who died in the care of the provincial hospitals, there may be estate files, which are listed alphabetically in the finding aid for the hospital records in the reading room at the Archives.

For many years, the developmentally handicapped were classed with the mentally ill, and so they may be found in the records of facilities at Woodstock, Orillia and Coburg.

Closer to home, the Homewood Sanitarium, which was founded as a private business venture in 1883, has deposited its papers at the Archives up to 1941. Researchers looking for Homewood materials should begin their enquiries at the office of the director in Guelph.

In short, there are a great many of these kind of records available at the Archives of Ontario, but access may be limited and finding the documents you want is not an easy road. As usual with interesting genealogical materials, perseverance and thoroughness are important.

To enquire about these materials, ask at the Archives of Ontario, 77 Grenville Street, Unit 300, Toronto M5S 1B3. They have a toll-free telephone line at 1-800-668-9933. Two recent pamphlets which introduce the Archives and family history research there are available at no charge.

(3 June 1997)

Ontario Local History Indexes
and Newfoundland Database

Picture yourself on a research trip. You have a couple of hours in a library far from home. You find a local history book and open it in anticipation of finding some relations inside.

But it does not have an index. What do you do? Spend an hour or more leafing through it? Give up?

I have done both, but if you want to get the most out of local histories, you have to spend time. On most research trips, you rarely have this.

The good news is that Sylvia Best of Peterborough has begun indexing Ontario local histories. Her indexes, produced as small booklets, are invaluable if they deal with areas that interest you.

Although she seems most interested (so far) in the Peterborough area, she has published indexes for books on Schomberg and Toronto, too. Locally, she has indexed the history of St. Vincent township and its schools.

Among her Kawartha area indexes are two for Norwood, and the standard history of Victoria County. Township histories are obvious candidates for the Best treatment, and she has already done Hope and Cavan (in old Durham County) and Emily (in Victoria). There are town histories too, for Tottenham, Newmarket and Peterborough itself.

James Scott's fine history of Huron County has a kind of index already, very general. Best has produced another, giving every name.

These indexes are quite straightforward, giving merely the names and pages. You will need to use them with the text itself at hand.

Researchers with great interests in an area will want to have the indexes at home to use. Others might bring these indexes to the attention of their local libraries or archives, who could provide them for use with their reference copies of the books involved.

And if your favourite unindexed history is not on Best's list yet, she might be willing to consider your suggestions. I understand she has plans to make this an ongoing business.

For a complete list of what's available and their prices, write to Sylvia Best at 577 Walnut Street, Peterborough K9H 2V3, or e-mail her at offcon@oncomdis.on.ca.

The Newfoundland and Labrador Genealogical Society's Cemetery and Parish Record Database is now available for searching. This will interest all those former Newfoundlanders in the area, especially in Cambridge. It now contains more than half a million names.

Search scope can be limited by region/community, religion, parish, type of event or date range. The search result lists all matches. For each non-member fee of $10, you get 50 references. The fee is not meant as a money-earner, but to defray costs of maintaining the database.

Since most researchers in Newfoundland have a good idea where their family lived, it may be possible to use the limiting factor and scoop in a giant handful of family references for this fee. The cemeteries on the database are from all over the province, and their aim is to include every cemetery there.

The Society advises, "For persons conducting a lot of research, membership in the NLGS is recommended". Membership halves the cost of the databases searches, and you also receive *The Newfoundland Ancestor*, one of Canada's best genealogical journals.

For details, consult the summer 1996 issue of *The Newfoundland Ancestor*, which is available at the Kitchener library's periodicals desk.

To institute a search, write to Index Search, Newfoundland and Labrador Genealogical Society, Colonial Building, Military Road, St. John's NF A1C 2C9. For more information, you can talk to Steve Delaney at sdelaney@voyager.newcomm.net.

(17 June 1997)

Subject List of the Columns, March 1993-June 1997

Columns included in this volume are marked with an asterisk (*)

1993

6 March	Getting Started
13 March	Family Stories Worth Recording*
20 March	Spelling of Family Names
27 March	Directories
3 April	Census Listings
10 April	Cemeteries
17 April	Obituaries*
24 April	Wills
1 May	Ontario Civil Registration
8 May	Using Libraries
15 May	Ships' Passenger Lists
22 May	Writing and Using Genealogical Queries*
29 May	National Archives of Canada*
5 June	Personal Ancestral File (software)
12 June	Buying Genealogical Supplies (Global)
19 June	Women's Institute Tweedsmuir Histories*
26 June	Dept. of Agriculture Records/age on census*
3 July	Census-assessment Records*
10 July	Finding Lost Relations (generally)
17 July	1858-1869 Marriage Records
24 July	Naturalization Records
31 July	Nature of Church Records
7 August	Religious Newspapers*
14 August	What Church Records to Look At*
21 August	Mary Bond's Canadian directories book/ Floreen Carter's Place Names of Ontario*
28 August	Cousinhood
4 September	Tax Records*
11 September	Using maps and atlases*
18 September	Nineteenth Century Weddings*
25 September	Waterloo County Churches: A Research Guide by Rosemary Ambrose (review)*
2 October	Move of Civil Registration Records to Ontario Archives
9 October	Archives of Ontario*

1993

16 October	Preparing for Overseas Trips*
23 October	Adoptees Search for Birth Parents*
30 October	Death Cards*
6 November	Research in Denmark and Holland
13 November	Patronymics and Family Nicknames*
20 November	Anglican Records*
27 November	English Records at LDS family history centers
4 December	Methodists in 19th century Ontario*
11 December	Scotland*
18 December	Telephone Directories*
24 December	Christmas in the 19th century
31 December	Family Crest Stores

1994

8 January	Divorce Records in Canada*
15 January	Narrative in Family Histories*
22 January	Genealogical Societies and their publications/ 1869-1872 vital records in Ontario
29 January	Planning research trips
5 February	Offers of instant family histories/ Two brothers with the same birthdate*
12 February	Canadian post office directories 1964-1977*
19 February	Alsace*
26 February	National Service Census, 1940/Poles in Wilno*
5 March	Civil Service List/Causes of Death*
12 March	Adoption Reunions (book review)
19 March	Irish Church Records (book review)*
26 March	Criminal Indictment Files at Archives of Ontario*
2 April	Loyalist Lineages of Canada (book review)*
9 April	Jail registers of Ontario*
16 April	Disappearing relatives (Bruce county)
23 April	Two books on Irish Research
30 April	WWI Soldiers' personal records
7 May	Unit War diaries WWI (follow-up to previous column)
14 May	Canada Gazette
21 May	How to Read Cemeteries

1994

28 May	Allen County Public Library, Fort Wayne, Indiana
4 June	Long Point Settlers (book review)
11 June	Irish Geography
18 June	Nova Scotia
25 June	Quakers in Ontario/Italian Emigration
2 July	Archives in Belfast and Dublin
9 July	Acadian names/Irish surveys
16 July	Large Genealogical Collections in Ontario Libraries and Archives (book review)
23 July	Methodist Episcopal baptisms in Niagara & Schleswig-Holstein*
30 July	Eastern Europe
6 August	Canadian Railway Records (book review)*
13 August	George Schweitzer and the War of 1812
20 August	Photo Works (photos on disk)*
27 August	Planning research: short cuts in family history (book review)
3 September	Bruce County society seminar: Bill Lawson
10 September	Books on Hessian mercenaries
17 September	Planning family reunions
24 September	Power Translator (software for languages)
1 October	Geoff Burtonshaw's Métis newsletter
8 October	Basic handbooks for English research*
15 October	PAF/Canada Tree/Temiskaming genealogical group
22 October	Mennonite Family History (magazine review)
25 October	Calendars*
1 November	Family Tree Maker (software)
8 November	Romanian genealogy
15 November	Ontario Genealogical Society
22 November	Zachary Cloutier, father of all French-Canadians*
29 November	Peel County*
6 December	Germans from Russia magazines
13 December	Genetics in genealogy
20 December	Christmas column (Taylor cookbook)
27 December	Scottish Genealogy Society publications

1995

3 January	Advice for beginners from GENEASSIST magazine*
10 January	Canadian valour awards/Managing a Genealogical project
17 January	Tracing your ancestors in Alberta (book review)
24 January	Emigration from Wuerttember & Baden
31 January	Dufferin County*
7 February	The Irish at Home and Abroad (magazine review)*
14 February	Choosing a professional genealogist
21 February	Phonedisc (CD-ROM review)
28 February	The Family Historian's Enquire Within (book review)*
7 March	Bruce County workshop: Brian Gilchrist
14 March	Following the Paper Trail (book review)
21 March	Black family history in Wellesley Township
28 March	OGS regional meeting in Harriston
4 April	Ontario marriage registrations 1869-1872
11 April	A family historian's guide to illness, disease and death (book review)*
18 April	Companies which photograph your ancestral village
25 April	Waterloo Historical Society annual volume
2 May	University archives and how they can help
9 May	Church of the Brethren records*
16 May	Latin American handbook/OGS Seminar 95
23 May	Looking at old photographs
30 May	Fraudulent family history books
6 June	World Tree (CD-ROM) and SKY version 4.0 (software)
13 June	Scanners
20 June	Regiment magazine (review)
27 June	University of Guelph Scottish collection*
4 July	Marsh Collection, Amherstburg*
11 July	Maritime History Archive, Memorial University*
18 July	Croatians in Canada (book review)
25 July	Fergus: a Scottish town (book review)
1 August	Presbyertian Church in Canada archives
8 August	Loiselle Index (Quebec marriages)*
15 August	Determining American citizenship
22 August	A genealogical riddle/ProCite (software review)
29 August	Finding a birth mother in Canada*

1995

5 September	National Library of Canada on the Internet*
12 September	Upper Canada Village Library
19 September	Upper Canada District Marriage Registers*
26 September	Brian Henley's books on Hamilton
3 October	Bruce & Grey Branch OGS's 25th anniversary
10 October	Federation of Genealogical Societies Conference, Seattle
17 October	A lecture on writing family booklets*
24 October	Wellington County Historical Society volume 1995
31 October	Hedges Query/More on Upper Canada Village
7 November	Quebec records and Cyprien Tanguay's work
14 November	Nicknames
21 November	Pioneers, a computer genealogy newsletter (review)
28 November	List of wedding guests/Caledonia (book review)
5 December	Finding cousins overseas*
12 December	German Life (magazine review)
19 December	Christmas column (Woodward family booklet)
26 December	Huber family discoveries

1996

2 January	BurMor (newspaper index publishers)*
9 January	Surprising autograph books and DNA
16 January	The task of the congregational historian (review)
23 January	Early German emigrants/Kawartha research centre
30 January	More Ontario marriage indexes/Quebec
6 February	GENTECH (computer conference review)
13 February	Lifetime expectancies of photographs*
20 February	Family History Monthly (magazine review)
27 February	How heavy, how much, how long (book review)*
5 March	Butler bicentenary/Franco-ontarian society library
19 March	Ephraim Weber's Letters Home (book review)*
2 April	OGS regional meeting/Preservation of documents
16 April	Jewish genealogy with Gary Mokotoff*
7 May	Commonwealth War Graves Commission*
21 May	Not a Problem NAP (software review)
4 June	Hay township history (book review)
18 June	Genealogy in Ontario; Here be Dragons! (book reviews)*

1996

2 July	State Library of Michigan*
16 July	FGS conference/Charlton Heston's genealogy
6 August	Oxford Companion to local and family history (book review)*
20 August	Wellington County
3 September	Erie Canal*
17 September	Civil Registration in Michigan and elsewhere
1 October	Bibliography of Glengarry County (book review)
15 October	One record is wrong, but which one?*
5 November	Glenbow Museum & Archives, Calgary*
19 November	Reading the census*
3 December	Donald Walker's discoveries in Tillsonburg*
17 December	Christmas column: Martha Barnhart's celebration*

1997

7 January	Baptismal records *
21 January	Ancestors (television series)
4 February	Saskatchewan Residents Index*
18 February	West Wawanosh township history (book review)
4 March	World Wide Cemetery website
18 March	Society of Genealogists, London*
1 April	OGS Seminar 97, Alliston
15 April	English genealogy bookshop*
6 May	Edmonton City Archives*
20 May	Grey County marriages (book review)/ Ottawa conference*
3 June	Medical records at the Archives of Ontario*
17 June	Indexes of Ontario local histories*

Index

Index

Index

Notes

Notes

Notes

Notes

Notes

Notes

Notes

_____

_____

_____

_____

_____

_____

_____

_____

_____

_____

_____

_____

Cover design by Umberto Micheli
in2DESIGN, Kitchener

Printed by Stewart Publishing & Printing
Markham, Ontario